Dirty Old River

Tom Emerson

DIRTY OLD RIVER

Edited by Sarah Handelman

for John

Framing Frank
12

The Monika Papers
34

Cutting Corners
54

Tolerance
60

Blue
66

Openings
68

From *Lieux* to Life
78

Dirty Old River
102

Gardens, Grids and Ghosts
120

Working at Home Like
Everyone Else
138

Juergen on a Plate
142

Tough Love
162

Dirty Old River is borrowed from the opening line of the Kinks' 'Waterloo Sunset', probably the best pop song about London and the most evocative three words about the city. In 2021, *Frieze* magazine commissioned artists and architects to share their favourite London buildings or public artworks, presumably to invite us back into the city after nearly two years of Covid-19 interior isolation. I chose the Thames rather than a single building or object. So many different walks in London could have served, but that short stretch of river I had walked alone, empty, during that daily hour of exercise sanctioned by the very government that partied carefree in Downing Street offered the perfect collision of made objects and infrastructures laid over a muddy geology. Far from getting boring, repetition only intensified how small events and details fitted into a bigger picture that has flowed in and out of the city for millennia. I had no idea that the continuous unfolding space of the river would be edited into tiny separate pins displayed across a digital map on the *Frieze* app. This is the first time the whole walk has been published as the intended drift of walking, talking, looking. All the other texts in this book have been, in some form, published before.

This collection, which spans nearly three decades, is neither consistent nor focused on a specific subject, location or discipline. It is naturally seen through the lens of architecture that shifts across different areas of interest. Like the projects of an architect in practice, it is as much the product of opportunity as it is a journey designed. All the essays were commissioned. They were preceded by many conversations and occasionally lectures where seeds were planted, but the shape of the book came from others.

Half the texts are dedicated to architecture or how architecture is produced. The other half touch on art practice, photography, literature, landscape and more generally the constructed world. Some are longer-form essays, spending time with subjects, while others are brief, more like vignettes or passing thoughts that may be developed in the future. If there is a guiding theme, it is an exploration of how and why things are made the way they are and what that tells us about being human. I remember someone saying that the half-Roman roofing tile is moulded by laying a soft sheet of clay across the thigh of its maker, giving it the characteristic conical tapering form that allows for the tiles to be laid in the overlapping pattern that will shed water off the roof. I doubt if the story is true, but it is exciting to think that every form and pattern around us is explicable by the body, geology, imagination and imitation, language, memory (especially when it fails), technology, economics – in short, by what we call culture. The texts are organised in a few broad categories starting with how things are made: Frank Gehry's early works exploding American framing, documented by Johan Dehlin, Monika Sosnowska's transformation of delicate paper objects into violent distortions of modernity and Nele Dechmann's architectural design for young footballers, by correspondence with Madagascan makers.

Then to drawing, the heart of architectural production, where marks on paper reveal far more than the technical instructions of what to build. Tolerance is key. Álvaro Siza's imagination and humanity can be traced through his construction drawings as much as the better known freehand sketches.

The oldest essay is also the newest. 'From *Lieux* to Life' follows the work of French writer Georges Perec as he moves through his epic attempt to capture the passing of time directly observed in the spaces of the city, to a wholly imagined world within a Parisian apartment block. What started as two separate texts in the 1990s that were reworked in the noughties has been brought together this year by a fortuitous Google search, now accidentally mirroring Perec's own aim to document how time changes places, memory and writing.

Two pieces towards the end lead directly to work by 6a architects. A story of Milton Keynes (there are many) in 'Gardens, Grids and Ghosts' ends in the building of MK Gallery, designed by our practice. And more recently the photographer Juergen Teller asked me to write a catalogue essay about his work for a retrospective we also designed at the Grand Palais Éphémère in Paris. In an early conversation he suggested writing about the photographs he has taken in the studio we designed for him some years before. As the deadline approached, and forgetting that conversation, he asked how I was getting on with writing about the process of designing the studio. The essay is an attempt to do both.

Perhaps it doesn't matter if what is done differs from what one originally set out to do. When the first of these pieces was written in 1997, I had set out to be an architect. I had not set out to write. There was an opportunity. And it seems fitting that those early texts were written about a novelist who writes about space and is spatial in his writing. It was like a primer before writing about the thing itself and established a habit of writing about architecture obliquely. I have found sideways glances, passing through another discipline or letting myself be guided by what is at hand, more fruitful and enjoyable than tackling the architecture head-on knowing I can't escape my profession. The texts that follow reveal all the biases of their times in subject and form. As we move closer to the present, reuse and repair, landscape and ecology have grown deeper roots in practice and in words. Once a building or landscape project is finished, it is only the beginning of its life in the world which is extremely unlikely to match its conception. Looking at how things are made and why, is really about how things grow, decay and keep on living.

Framing Frank

Infatuation

I landed at LAX with the sceptical eye of a non-car-owning European already in thrall with NY but ready to appreciate the Southern California sunshine, some Europhilic Modern marvels and ignore everything else, especially the drive. But within twenty minutes on the appropriately named 'I' northbound, just past the first hills lined with nodding donkeys pumping the oil that fuels LA, I was under the Angel's spell. *Another Brit loves LA. What is it with you?*[1] complained a New Yorker a couple of decades later, infatuation undiminished. *Not still reading Banham?* The exact reasons are not easy to explain, but they might have something to do with the feeling of freedom offered by the absence of known bearings (geographic, architectural, civic, landscape or infrastructural), or the bricolage assembly of disparate macro and micro elements that Colin Rowe wrote about Rome, LA and London,[2] or the rejection of grand urban gestures of any kind. LA is specific, unruly and hybrid in the extreme. The irregular collision of styles, types, uses, scales and influences is never tamed by the grids laid across the city. In fact, the grid only heightens the irrepressible tectonics into which twenty-five million people have settled. LA is tolerant, even if tolerance comes with extreme inequality.

Tornado

To visit Frank Gehry's house is to visit LA in miniature. Late morning, in spring 2003, we descend on Washington and 22nd Street, an unsuspecting corner of genteel suburbia. Under respectable pitched eaves, pink weatherboarding rises neatly. The storm begins low, at ground level, with irregular steps leading to the front door tucked behind a screen of galvanised corrugated steel and chain-link fencing that tilts like an insolent cap. But it is around the corner that Gehry and LA (OK, Santa Monica...) deal cupid's arrow. That rooflight. *I could build that*, I thought, looking at the simple softwood cube covered in glass. And I probably could, but I could never have dropped it into place at that jaunty angle. In fact, the whole suburban material palette wrapped around the house appears like a tornado that has stopped dead, mid-flight, like a Buster Keaton movie paused. Corrugations and fencing enmeshed with agaves and timber framing from any nearby construction site swirl around the 1920s original. There you have it, Gehry and LA, so normal, so ordinary, so unexpected, so simple, so complex. The cheap, the typical, the everyday; the architecture, empty plots, suburban yards, basketball courts Downtown or tennis courts in the Hills. Stock products piled high in builders' merchants and Home Depot. There begins the journey Gehry made in the late 1970s, a trajectory that meanders south from Santa Monica to Venice in the 1980s and out into the world. Forty years later, the photographer and architect Johan Dehlin documented those curious but crucial early steps to global architectural fame.

Play It As It Lays

See that? said a Los Angeles contractor as he stood on a site overlooking the city, sweeping his hand across the vista, *All made with a Skilsaw.* I've always liked construction site aphorisms. They contain the right mix of truth, romance and BS. And if there is any truth, it is that the Skilsaw stands for all the saws commonly used by everyday builders and amateurs in the story of American framing, representing a kind of universal vernacular – open, democratic, efficient, entrepreneurial. The romance is that the freedom of Los Angeles is built of honest and repeating domestic units, timber frames assembled ad infinitum. The BS is just BS. The early buildings designed by Frank Gehry may well be the perfect synthesis of all three.

Banham suggests Los Angeles has no *public monuments worth visiting*.[3] The contractor would not be offended because his frame is the beat of the city. The tourist on the other hand seeks exceptions. This is where Gehry comes in. The exceptional is the background, straight, turned up, sideways, rolled over, but the frame never misses a beat, telescoping the vastness of the American landscape through the grid of the city until you are nailing cheap lumber in two-foot increments. The sinuous highway gliding over the city is the melody over the beat.

In *Play It As It Lays*,[4] Joan Didion's Maria survives living by the beat, dressing fast because *to pause was to throw herself into unspeakable peril* in order to get onto the freeway. *Once she was on the freeway and had maneuvered her way to the fast lane she turned on the radio at high volume and she drove. ... Again and again she returned to an intricate stretch just south of the interchange where successful passage from Hollywood onto Harbor required a diagonal move across four lanes of traffic. On the afternoon she finally did it without once braking or once losing the beat on the radio she was exhilarated, and that night slept dreamlessly.* Like Maria, Gehry finds traction in the everyday momentum of LA. Her beat is kept by *the touch of the accelerator* in the Corvette. His is in the repetition of softwood studs keeping time as structures rise obliquely but fall in sync. The rhythm in the humble stud becomes spatial and social.

Cool School[5]

One of the great myths about Gehry is his likeness to an artist. His intuitive sense of space sketched in whirling lines only he understands is published in expensive doorstop volumes.[6] It is a myth promoted by the man himself, driving around LA with Sydney Pollack filming at his side in 2007,[7] talking art and artists. But this is not the real LA, nor perhaps even the real Gehry. It is a Hollywood retelling of stories he has told so many times they gain a second truth. More LA BS but not the helpful kind. In fact, all this arthouse dressing-up does Gehry's work a disservice. It promotes the idea that all of his projects are somehow conceived, and should be seen, as artworks. And while Gehry has been close to artists throughout his life, the meaning of his early works is above all in the architectural and urban realm of everyday LA. It is what they do for users, how they celebrate the craziness of LA, how they bring consistency and duration to a place that cares little for either. Gehry's projects make sense of a senseless place, *genus*-LA.

Rather than *Gehry the artist*, better to see him as the cuckoo's egg in the architectural nest. Despite the absence of explicit politics or theory, he steals critical bites from the overactive theories of American architecture. More than once, he was adopted by the scribes of Deconstruction of the 1980s and 90s for his abrupt and oblique geometric shifts before a more general absorption into the fold of postmodernism – a better fit, although I doubt Gehry cares much for either. If neither term is helpful in describing the early projects, it would be wrong to think of his work as without culture. The informal ease of Gehry's imagination covers deep and wide-ranging architectural knowledge. Unfinished framing and other gestures in fencing et al. were found, not invented. The west coast artworld harvested what the city naturally produced. Construction sites, gas stations and cars offered readymade forms and materials, which, if they were not made into artworks themselves, were in the studios that produced them. Gehry's work absorbs these found images into the raw language of construction and space alongside architectural references without rhetorical fanfare. Close to home, he draws on Schindler's 1922 houses on Kings Road and then, through Rossi, plenty more from Italy in later works. The originality here is one only architecture can contrive. It is spatial and useful, scaled to body and city.

Photography

It is a strange lacuna in a career with artistic ambitions that there is no singular discernible photographic oeuvre to represent Gehry's projects in LA. This is even more surprising in a city which exists as much on film and photography as it does in reality. Mid-century modernism in California is barely conceivable without the photographs by Julius Shulman. And if the depiction of a hyper-stylised Case Study House 22 cantilevering over LA is anathema to the directness of Gehry's early buildings, his artworld friends had viable alternatives. They were photographing the same conditions of urban debris beyond the gaze of high modernism or Hollywood that provided the architect's palette. Ed Ruscha's small artist books of the late 1960s and 70s on gas stations, swimming pools, car parks, empty lots, apartment buildings and the unfolding Sunset Boulevard capture the city in all its extraordinary ordinariness. His images are precise, off axis just enough to feel the camera is in hand. At the same time, Lewis Baltz took a more detached and abstract look at industrial suburbs, turning prosaic industrial blandness into exercises in pure form.

The work of both Ruscha and Baltz (and probably many others) was highly visible in the LA art scene of the 1970s. And while Gehry was part of it, designing and collaborating with several among them, photographic representation does not have the consistency of the projects themselves despite, or maybe because of, the number of named/famed photographers[8] who recorded it (including Shulman). Instead, from the safety of his car, Gehry turned his gaze to the city fringes, photographing unfinished industrial structures and materials stacked in builders' yards waiting to find their place somewhere/anywhere in LA. His gaze is closer to Didion's Maria: *Sometimes the freeway ran out, in a scrap metal yard in San Pedro or somewhere no place at all where the flawless burning concrete just stopped, turned into common road, abandoned construction sheds rusting beside it.* Gehry's images capture a reality banished from the fantasy of Los Angeles that Hollywood makes and remakes. They show his curiosity casually, without the rigour of Ruscha or Baltz,[9] and without the theoretical drive of Denise Scott Brown and Robert Venturi on Main Street. His focus is on collecting forms and materials, not in pictorial effect.

Gehry's photographs of LA from the early 1970s are absent from the first and, to my mind, best monograph of his early works, published by Rizzoli in 1985.[10] More than three hundred pages packed with projects are laid out parallel to the binding like a calendar or centrefold.

An opening essay by Germano Celant – the art critic who named Arte Povera[11] – dissects the *anatomy* of Gehry's low-fi *organisms*,[12] city and house in one. What follows is a treasure trove of images and drawings of all the projects to date, from the smallest to the largest, built and not. Many are now forgotten or demolished, sometimes both.[13] The book reflects the remarkable consistency of Gehry's buildings and the freedom of LA. Drawings and images are rough, conveying the information quickly with plenty of tolerance, before moving on to the next.[14] Nearly forty years have passed. Gentrification has followed – at least in the once open and unfinished neighbourhoods that allowed these modest projects to grow. Long gone are the empty lots that breathed fresh air into the city grid. Some of the more famous works have been rephotographed, gaining in brightness but with it a loss of innocence. Gehry's seminal Ron Davis House (1971) was destroyed by a wildfire in 2018.

Johan Dehlin photographed Los Angeles and five Gehry buildings in 2015 thanks to a small scholarship from a Swedish foundation. He spent three months getting to know the city and rediscovering this family of buildings that now exist in the shadow of Gehry's later iconic fame. Dehlin's photographic eye stands in stark contrast to the architecture; he is calm and still where Gehry is restless. The passing of time stands in equally stark contrast to a city that refuses to age; the orange cast of new Douglas fir studs and plywood that saturated the early images has faded to a darker brown. Dehlin's gaze is firmly indebted to Bernd and Hilla Becher who photographed the end of European industry at the same time the Cool School documented LA's becoming. Devotees of the Neue Sachlichkeit, the Bechers saw impartially, objectively, in black and white. They waited patiently outside the scene, sometimes for days, for the right even light to fall, isolating involuntary monuments from landscapes of extraction. Unlike the Bechers, Dehlin's images erase neither context nor the author, but they do allow a gaze to linger, to turn the frenzy into still life. And unlike the Düsseldorf School led by the Bechers, Dehlin's images welcome the sun, saturation and accumulation.

The first weeks of the trip were occupied with the city, capturing what LA offered for free, as access to Gehry buildings proved elusive apart from Gemini GEL gallery and print studio, which is open to the public and famously welcoming. As the weeks passed into months, a portrait of LA emerged: the grid laid over seismic topography, its avenues of palms, broken pavements, signs and eclectic architectural compositions. Email requests to visit the houses remained unanswered. But just as the return to Europe approached, owners opened their doors to Dehlin and his camera. At Indiana Avenue, a young entrepreneur has made a tech HQ. The Benson House has been lovingly restored to near original spec by the new owners. Jane Spiller and Mr Norton still owned the homes they commissioned four decades ago.

In the early houses Gehry captured an essential and readymade LA vernacular. Dehlin, too, captures the spaces as both found and lived. Furniture, skateboards, marketing props and artworks occupy the architecture unselfconsciously, naturally. The interiors are darker and more intimate than before. What were once exercises in speed and balance, of elements tumbling within and around one another, have come to rest. The stair that fell from the sky and twisted against the plan has settled like a stone dislodged in a ruin that found repose long ago. While the formality of Dehlin's images is in many respects foreign to Gehry's nervous energy, his pictures create new fragments, new spaces in which the architecture is reinvented. Like a good jazz musician, the photographer catches LA marginally behind the beat.

Objects and Caves

Dehlin's exteriors present closed sculptural objects in series of two or three standing in a dispersed urban landscape. Not in a Becher-like sense of splendid isolation, but still, standing apart, different and incomplete. The portrait format helps. The street is not the thing. The interiors, on the other hand, are cavernous. If there are views out, they mainly frame sky or are partially obscured by a lazy curtain. Only the Norton House throws itself open towards the beach in the form of a lookout tower protected by shutters on three sides, ready to close at any moment.

The three volumes at Indiana Avenue are, similarly, simple variations on a closed timber box. Always the same, always unique. The first, from the south, is the most generously fenestrated by an exaggerated bay window chamfering the corner. The second, clad in raw plywood, replies with a fireplace and chimney, which in the interior is nothing but a nook. The third breaks the box from the top. Out of place and out of scale, a stair cascades obliquely through the roof, dividing the corner and punching outward from the otherwise orthogonal volume with a kind of crow-stepped gable that produces the famous interior ceiling of densely gridded structure. That's LA. The interiors of the three structures are defined by a main space that matches the given form, articulated by smaller variations. Bridges and bay in the first, chimney-turned-closet in the second, baroque ceiling to finish. Regardless of the exuberant cuts and folds that let light and sun fall in all the right places over today's tech residents, the spaces are mainly enclosed, with enough edges, textures and shadows to create worlds unto themselves.

A few blocks north, the Spiller House is at once simpler and more complex. Two houses, separated by a pocket garden: a minor two-storey for rent and a major four-storey volume for the owner, Jane Spiller. Once a collaborator in the Eames studio, she commissioned Gehry with a budget barely sufficient for the build. He accepted under the condition of design freedom.[15] That freedom reveals itself in surprisingly restrained timber-framed volumes clad in corrugated steel like the garages that line the narrow streets leading to Venice Beach. A few offset windows placed flush in the facade so nonchalantly that the framing runs across uninterrupted behind glass. Within, the studwork lobby at ground level unwinds upwards from small to large, from dark to light, the tornado of suburban debris around the Gehry House turned inside out. Within the controlled enclosure, the interior swirls, like climbing the inside of a steeple. The Spiller House is a silver micro-tower reaching for, but never matching, the height or sway of the surrounding palms. Somewhat ahead of their time, the slanted array of solar panels is gone today.

The character of construction is laconic as ever, but the spaces are made more precise thanks to Jane Spiller's insistence on selecting longer timber sections than standard. From some angles the double-height living room with balcony echoes the Eameses' own famous interior. Details in Dehlin's photograph show the architect's fingerprints: an external stair cuts across a door with little regard to form or the resident's unsuspecting head, while in the floor above, the door is trimmed to the descending stringer. Neither necessary, both gently accommodating, tolerant, in their own way. In Dehlin's view of the roof, Jane Spiller emerges from the retracted skylight. Dressed in white and with her long silver hair, she mirrors the otherworldliness of the home she commissioned back in 1980.

Of the five projects photographed by Dehlin, Gemini GEL, Indiana Avenue and the Spiller House can be seen as the end of something while the Benson and Norton houses represent a beginning. The difference is subtle and almost certainly not consciously planned by Gehry. The first three translate the Santa Monica mindset into spatial and sculptural experiments while remaining true to ground-zero LA's commercial vernacular. Benson and Norton start a journey to other places. The former, more or less contemporary with Indiana Avenue, is the bridge to elsewhere. Form, space and materials are easily recognisable, but they also announce the one-room-one-building period[16] that Gehry would explore for many years, first in houses then in larger projects. Until this point, the spatial fragmentation in stairs and mezzanines was internal or tightly tied to the main volume. At the Benson House, these elements – still made and finished in the ubiquitous framing and roofing felt – start to assert their independence. At Norton, volumetric fragmentation unleashes new architectural elements and colour. Pastel ceramics and paint are sampled from surf shops, bong boutiques, t-shirt stalls and beach culture in full bloom. Chain-link fencing is superseded by a primitive portico of natural log à la Laugier below a lifeguard lookout, long before *Baywatch* made them famous. The rest is sunwashed fun piled high. But the interiors remain true to type, as intimate and serene as any, the march of framing unbroken.

The beauty of Dehlin's images is how they capture ends and beginnings in shared middle age. It is amazing, and a testament to Gehry and his clients, that these buildings have survived so well and remained so intact in a place built on obsolescence. Of course, they have been repaired and refurbished but that, too, should be encouraged today.

Celant wrote in 1985, *They are like paraphrases of the city and the landscape, with each building and individual village – a summation of independent contrasting entities.*[17] LA has changed a great deal since then, these five buildings very little. Gehry may have created the kind of rare place that opposes Baudelaire's regret, *the form of a city changes faster, alas! than a mortal's heart.*[18]

Change of Climate

A city built on oil extraction and consumption, Los Angeles may prove to be the last refuge of western excess. Six hundred thousand houseless citizens seek shelter below the wealthiest McMansions. Fire always a threat. Water always at risk. Los Angeles is not the place to go for guidance on climate change. Yet among the grotesque contradictions, early Gehry buildings provide some reason for hope.

The house in Santa Monica is the laboratory from which Gehry would extract his means to the new, and even (the mental stretch acknowledged) demonstrate a mindset fit for an ecological architecture. A modest rehearsal of what needs to be done today: reuse, optimised renewable materials and building envelopes with enough enclosure for naturally stable environments. In these five projects, there is refreshingly no distinction between the new, the extension or the refurbishment. The starting point is what is there, whether fencing around an empty lot or an existing building. Gehry's own house, Gemini GEL gallery and the slightly later Temporary Contemporary absorb the existing without question or fuss. They are neither fetishised as monuments nor treated carelessly but accepted with cool empathy. Careful stripping at Santa Monica reveals the bones without compromising the original. Gemini GEL gallery barely changes the original car showroom on Melrose Ave. The accommodating spirit towards the found naturally locates itself in the extension. The ubiquity of Gehry's material palette in LA lets him grow new spaces onto older structures like one grafts a new rose onto an old root. Additions are simple in conception and construction yet complex in outcome. At Gemini GEL, Gehry adds a two-storey square beside the original. Inside the square, another, slightly rotated. The intersection of the two timber grids provides all the spaces needed to place stairs or bring top light into a print studio below. While every space is simple and stable, the whole remains porous.

And what might be good for an extension can be turned towards the newbuild. Thanks to modest budgets and the long tradition of American framing that optimised material and labour, a maximum spatial outcome in volume and expression is produced with a minimum of material. The predominant material is regular Douglas fir sawn studwork and plywood. If it was not sustainably produced in the 1970s and 80s, there are certainly renewable alternatives today. Once the carpentry has sketched out space and form, the frames are clad in roofing felt, corrugated steel, thin stucco or left unfinished. They are not insulated. Southern Californian climate does not require much heating, and summer heat is easily expelled with air conditioning (no environmental points there). But these structures could be insulated easily, without compromising the architecture. What would Gehry have done with some organic fibrous insulation in the mix? I would love to know the embodied carbon of an Indiana Avenue or Benson in relation to an Eames, Koenig or Neutra. A steel frame wrapped in glass like the Case Study Houses is unimaginable now, but any of these early Gehry projects could be rebuilt as a model in low-energy construction. This is unfair, I know. It is measuring LA by standards and units that did not exist at the time of its making. And in our age of science, this can only score highly in feeling. Still, it's a start. Well remembered, well digested, embodied and lived to the full, they may be more than useful today and for decades to come. The new commons they are not, but the means are there for a common hand.

1. Reyner Banham, *Los Angeles: The Architecture of Four Ecologies* (New York: Harper & Row, 1971).
2. Colin Rowe and Fred Koetter, *Collage City* (Cambridge, MA: The MIT Press, 1978).
3. Reyner Banham asking Ed Ruscha what is worth seeing in Los Angeles in the car park of Tiny Naylor's drive-in restaurant on Sunset Boulevard. Ruscha answers, distracted, *Maybe... gas stations, maybe...*
   RB: *Just gas stations?*
   ER: *Well maybe any kind of edifice that has to do with the car...*
   RB: *Mmhuh...*
   ER: *...and gas stations is one of them.*
   RB: *Yeah, but what are the particular virtues of these buildings?*
   ER: *Well, the fact that they can just knock them up, put them together in just three days...*
   RB: *Mmhuh...*
   ER: *...or less. Sometimes it takes longer to tear down an old building than it does to put up a new one.*
   RB: *Right!*
   ER: *They're streamlined, everything about them is streamlined, that's what I like.*
   RB: *And is standardisation a virtue?*
   ER: *Oh yeah, definitely. I like the fact that they can put something up and get right to business and you know that they don't want to lose any time.*
   RB: *Yes but from the observing visitor's point of view, it means you can visit the same building in nine hundred different locations.*
   ER: *Yeah but you're not sure if it will be in the same location when you come back again next year.* 'Reyner Banham Loves Los Angeles', BBC, 1972, www.youtube.com/watch?v=WlZoNbC-YDo&ab_channel=TylerGoss.
4. Joan Didion, *Play It As It Lays* (New York: Farrar, Straus & Giroux, 1970), 15–18.
5. *The Cool School*, 2008, directed by Morgan Neville, written by Kristine McKenna and Morgan Neville, narrated by Jeff Bridges.
6. Too much attention is paid to Gehry's sketches at the expense of construction drawings that set out not only spatial, dimensional and technical descriptions but more modestly carry the very spirit of the work in every stroke, which in turn finds its answer in the cut of a saw, the striking of a nail, the making of the house. The same could be said of Gehry's architectural twin, Álvaro Siza, who also faces a sun setting over the ocean of the west-facing coast and whose angelic sketches are celebrated for their intuitive virtuosity. But it is in the working drawings that one finds the greatest inventions and humanity.
7. *Sketches of Frank Gehry*, directed by Sydney Pollack, 2007.
8. The Getty Research Institute digital collection lists thousands upon thousands of images.
9. Gehry's documentary photographs of LA have, as far as I know, only been published once in the catalogue of the exhibition at the Centre Pompidou, 2014–15. *Frank Gehry* (Paris: Éditions Centre Pompidou, 2014), 50–53.
10. Peter Arnell and Ted Bickford, eds., *Frank Gehry: Buildings and Projects* (New York: Rizzoli, 1985).
11. Celant first coined the term as part of his 1967 exhibition *Arte Povera – Im Spazio* at Galleria La Bertesca in Genoa.
12. Germano Celant, 'Reflections on Frank Gehry', in *Frank Gehry: Buildings and Projects*, 6.
13. Among the now famous projects is a series of temporary pavilions built for music and theatre dotted around Venice Beach that sow the seeds of the spatial and material invention documented here. The biggest and most lavish is the outdoor concert hall made for the Hollywood Bowl of giant cardboard sono-tubes (1970). While this wonderful structure no longer exists, it is the key location in *Columbo*, series 2, episode 2, 'Etude in Black', 1972.
14. *Frank Gehry: Buildings and Projects*. The last pages of the book list all projects to date. An unillustrated 'Ed Ruscha House, 1977', is recorded here, but I am not aware that it has ever been published or listed again. One wonders what that might have been...
15. See Mildred Friedman, *Frank Gehry: The Houses* (New York: Rizzoli, 2009), 155–61.
16. Throughout the 1980s and 1990s, Gehry would design a series of houses where each room was defined by a single building aggregating into a three-dimensional collage. See the Winton Guest House, 1983–85.
17. Celant, 'Reflections on Frank Gehry', 5.
18. Charles Baudelaire, 'The Swan', in *The Flowers of Evil* (1857).

24   *Framing Frank*

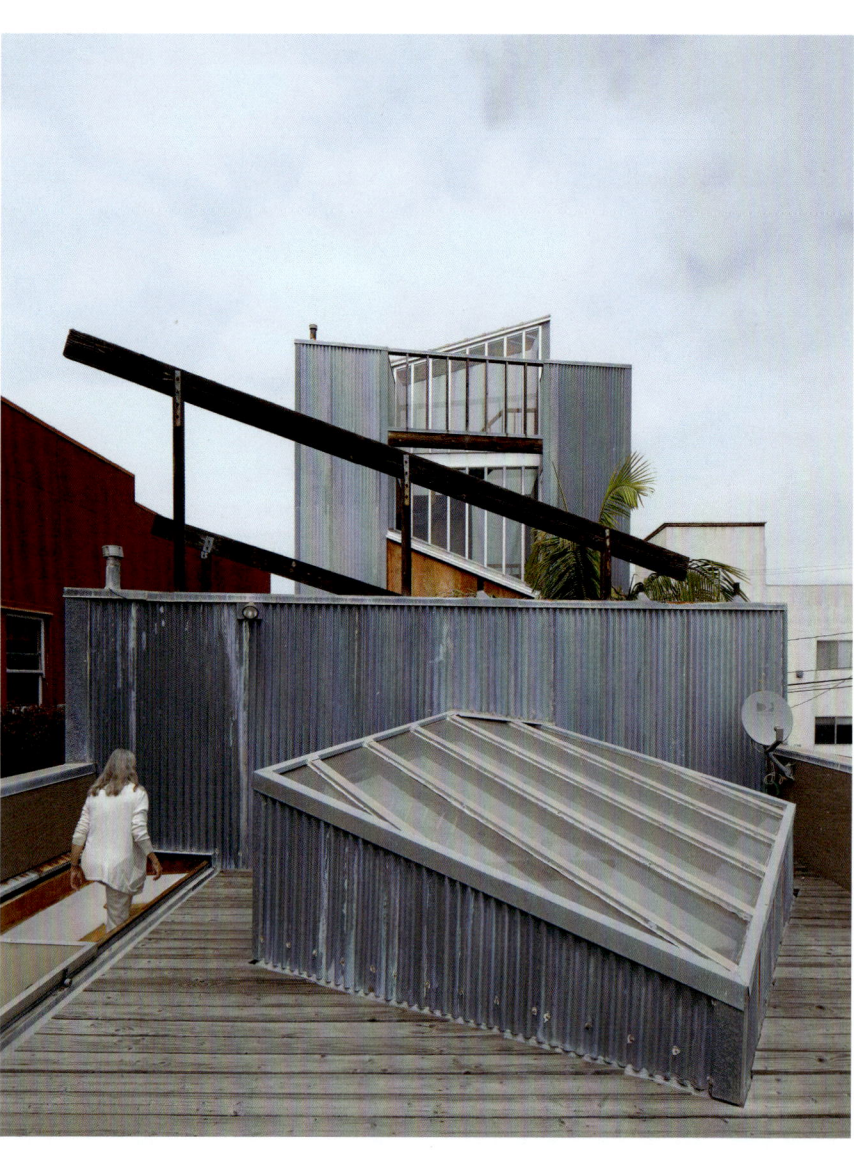

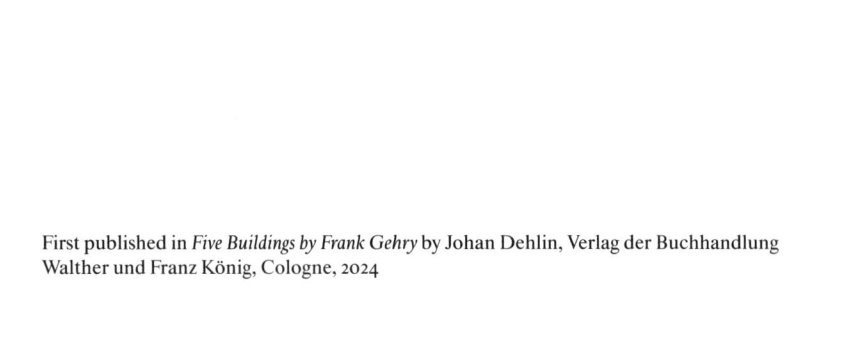

First published in *Five Buildings by Frank Gehry* by Johan Dehlin, Verlag der Buchhandlung Walther und Franz König, Cologne, 2024

The Monika Papers

Part I
Hanging by a Paperclip

The tools of the trade start with a thirty-centimetre steel ruler, scalpel, set square or triangle, cutting mat, a thin, hard-ish mechanical pencil for discreetly marking, some glue and, of course, stiff paper or card. The modelmaker may choose to expand this kit: rulers of fifteen centimetres to help with the fiddly little cuts, and those of fifty centimetres for the longer kind. The scalpel must be extremely sharp and requires a stock of fresh blades. There are plenty of craft knives with adjustable, snap-off blades, but for the experienced modelmaker the classic Johnson & Johnson brass medical scalpel is the tool of choice. Stainless steel set squares for cutting right angles come in all sizes. Cutting must always follow a steel edge. A modelmaker who cuts along a plastic edge is not to be trusted. Glue is UHU for general use, PVA for strength and superglue for speed.

Most of the models by the Polish artist Monika Sosnowska are made of paper and card. The paper or card model is the closest modelmaking gets to drawing. Not only do the tools come closest to those of a drafting set, but the process is guided by a highly sensitive dialogue between fingertip and eye, a form of fine motor communication that is shared with drawing and other dextrous tasks such as sewing, surgery and sleights of hand. It may seem a kind of paradox that Sosnowska uses such a sensitive technique and fragile material to build her models given that these delicate objects later take form in structural steel, but the artist's choices are related to the fact that she uses such architectural methods against the production of architecture. The material rupture between model and work anticipates the transformation between what Sosnowska creates and the world she extracts them from. Nothing is ever as it seems. Just as paper is not steel, Sosnowska's stair, beam, window or handrail are not architecture. And under cover of architectural elements, Sosnowska twists and bends stories of hope and regret from the debris of modernist utopia.

Architectural models rarely have a direct material relationship to the buildings they represent. This is partly because unlike sculpture, architecture is not materially consistent. Modernism tried very hard to make substance primary – aka truth to materials – where what you see is what it is. But this is a fiction, just one of the many promises and myths that made it so effective at casting the world anew. The white walls of the Bauhaus hide traditional brickwork, just as the steel I-sections on Mies van der Rohe's American facades – one of the many subjects of

Sosnowska's gaze – are not structural. For a while at least, from the 1920s until the oil crisis, the myth of the new was worth pursuing. In both the West and the East, modernist rationality served multiple social and political ends. But even if a work of architecture is conceived in terms of a primary substance like stone, concrete, steel, glass or timber, there is still a huge number of secondary and tertiary materials corralled to make it a usable building: damp-proofing, breather membranes, insulation, silicone and all the gloopy mixtures to seal a habitable space from the increasingly angry vicissitudes of nature. The promise of modernism to make the world better – and its inevitable failure to do so – is Sosnowska's subject.

The architectural model has many motives. For Sosnowska, the journey from model to finished work turns on a simple but radical material shift in which physical properties are inverted only to be restored by perception: we believe that paper can be, will be, steel. Using construction documents, she makes scale models in card – perhaps very much like the authors of the original structures – which she then, I assume, presses and pulls until a new form emerges. These are extremely precise distortions measured by touch as much as by the eye. The new form promises a new reality just like those that Brassaï produced by folding and rolling bus tickets into involuntary sculptures. Fingertip subversions of the everyday objects of industrial society.

If the models are a first re-enactment of the purity of modernist visions, then the second re-enactment in her process – the fabrication of the works in steel – is altogether more violent. Once Sosnowska's model is made, the full-size steel fragments are fabricated. This is true for the original buildings in the world that provoke the works, and the replicas reproduced by Sosnowska that are subjected to stress and distortion. Both are made of small parts that are assembled and welded into three-dimensional structures of slender steel angles or L-sections. The assembly is engineered to optimise their collective strength with the lightest means. New sculptural form and space emerges as the objects are twisted and bent. Every piece of angle distorts in its own unique way, in continuous communication with the next element it is bound to. The paper model is the reference for finding form, but reality imposes its own corrections. This is a dangerous process. The elasticity of steel threatens to spring a violent return.

Simulating architecture in a consistent material is a rhetorical exercise. Some models are made to seduce and convince. Postwar cities, for example, were modelled in pale wood and admired from above as architects explained the beautiful new worlds to politicians. From a bird's-eye

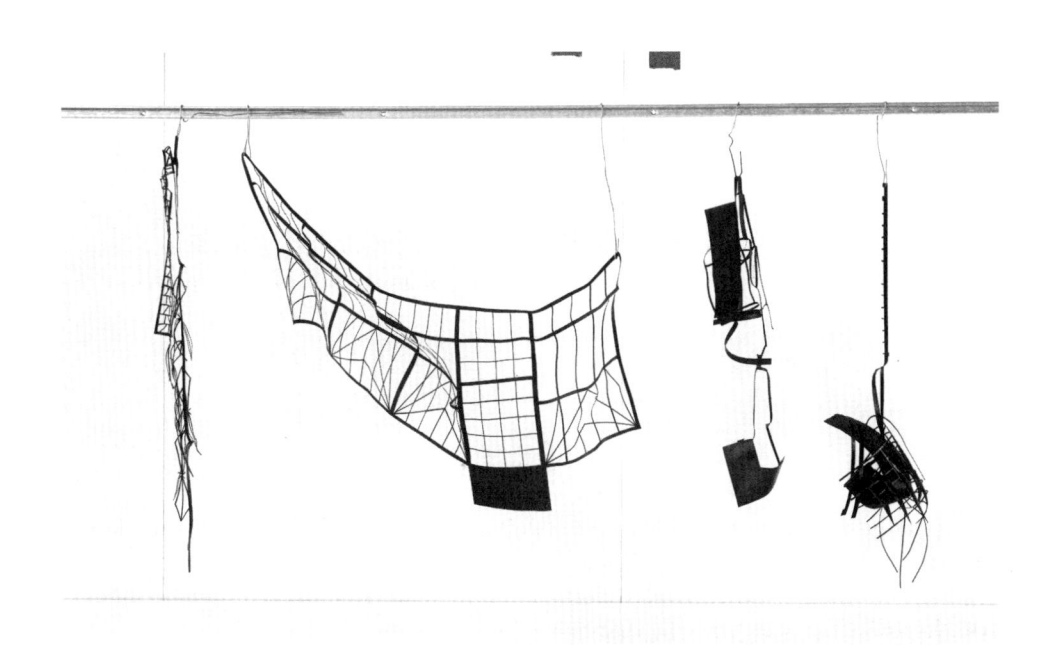

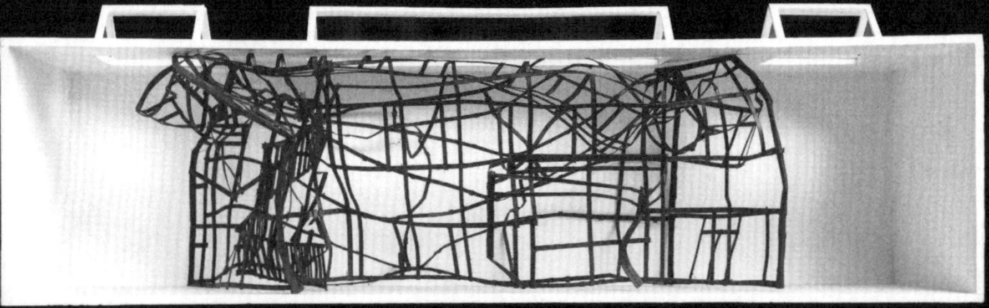

view their organisation would have given an impression of clarity and control, only to be reinforced by the model's material purity. The pale wood of postwar planning has since been replaced by backlit acrylic blocks that suggest the glow of profit. These are now ubiquitous around the world, where every luminous cube is a real estate opportunity, including those in post-socialist cities like Sosnowska's native Warsaw. What is messy, noisy, chaotic and subject to all the caprices of human nature in the street is rendered reassuringly calm, abstract, distant.

But preceding – and often happening alongside the more legible examples – are working models, those made to conceive the work. Often roughly assembled, they are produced by architects to create and test spaces, to see where light can fall and bounce around, where materials are substituted with precise intent. They come together at the speed of thought and carry all the errors, corrections, uncertainties and discoveries generated by the design process. The same basic tools still apply, only now wielded with abandon, as this object is not for public consumption.

Sosnowska uses the means of architectural modelmaking but subverts the ends. Many of her models are made of card and would fit comfortably on an ordinary working table alongside the tools described above. I have seen some elegantly arranged in the artist's studio on Dieter Rams's modular Vitsoe shelving, yet another brief encounter with a modernist architect. The most enduring impression of Sosnowska's models are ribbons of black-painted paper bending and twisting fragments of modern architecture into new disobedient forms and spaces, but it is by no means the only one. The first models, dating from the early 2000s, are the most spatial and architectural. Doors within doors within doors and corridors suggesting an infinite perspective. Faceted architectural aliens cranking their way around a suite of white cube galleries. The subversion of spaces and thresholds is made with the same control as the buildings that host them. Model and site are one.

But in Sosnowska's exhibition *1:1* in the Polish pavilion at the Biennale di Venezia in 2007, the model of the work and the context take separate paths. A replica of a modernist pavilion in Poland, slightly larger than the exhibition space in Venice, is crushed down to fit, the structure bending inwards and outwards. Both the card model and the 1:1 steel structure buckle to find their new diminished form inside the top-lit gallery. Paper and steel relent. The distress is shared, but the model and the work come to rest in specific and different ways as autonomous objects, related in intent but separated by physical properties and scale. Sosnowska's model does not replicate form in miniature like an architectural model; it sketches a transformation that only reality will deliver. Steel, after all, does not behave like card. Fingertip pinching and the pressing of fine strips of card glued together in the form of a building cannot be scaled up. The model succumbs to the infinitely small pressures applied by the hands that hold the scalpel, while the real work is welded by skilled fabricators. With the help of winches, chains and presses, it is stressed into disorderly shape. Force, however, does not follow a linear scale. A model like Sosnowska's, made at one-twentieth of the size of the work, will require hundreds if not thousands of times the force applied by the hand to distort the steel at full scale.

Scale is also mutable. The works themselves range in size from objects in a room to the room itself and from there to a building which may or may not fit into another and then to whole urban set pieces such as the facade of Mies van der Rohe's Lake Shore Drive tower. Yet the models rarely transcend the desk or shelf. The model for *Tower* (2014) is casually rolled up like a newspaper to lie alongside larger models of smaller objects. Here, the architect's strict taxonomy of scale is obsolete.

Despite sharing many materials and processes, the artist's and architect's models communicate opposite intentions. The architect will absorb and abstract a multitude of materials into a single component. A brick wall, for example, can be represented by parallel sheets of card made into a thin box to represent thickness. Windows are often suggested by simply leaving a void in the solid wall. Architectural models reduce the complexity of building into a suggestion of space and form through solid and void. Occasionally, the more technical architect will add detail to beams or trusses, but the simplification remains. Sosnowska's models, on the other hand, use the same number of components as the works they represent. The thinness of paper strips naturally falls enmeshed, textile-like. The works in structural steel will destroy any such ease.

Nevertheless, the model and the work enjoy an intimate relationship. The wilting leaves of spiral stairs are easily recognisable in both. Filigree strips of card representing window frames dangle like documents passing through an office shredder. Some models are freestanding, like the ones on the studio shelves. Others are suspended, letting gravity complete the modelmaker's gentle pull. Only the unfolded paperclip from which they hang reveals their true lightness. And while they are often painted black, in unison with their full-size steel sibling, some are left raw, like the architect's working model, with the pencil lines and small wrinkles visible where the flat sheet of card bends. Some have thick card bases, like proto plinths, marked with generating geometry or simply with the scale 1:10. Some are mounted on boards to suggest a wall of an unknown room.

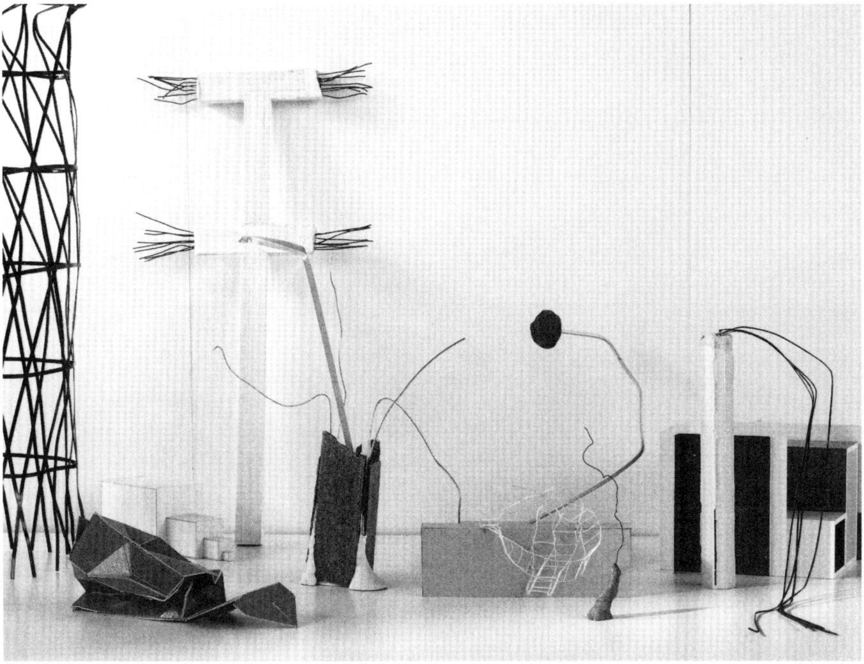

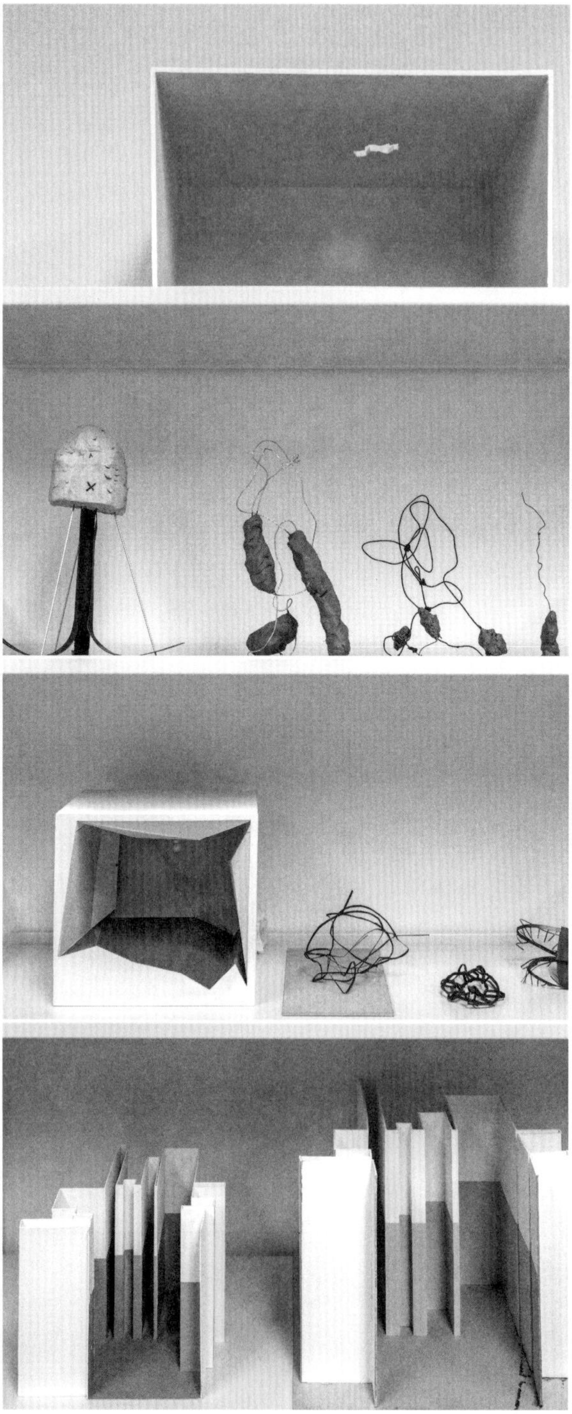

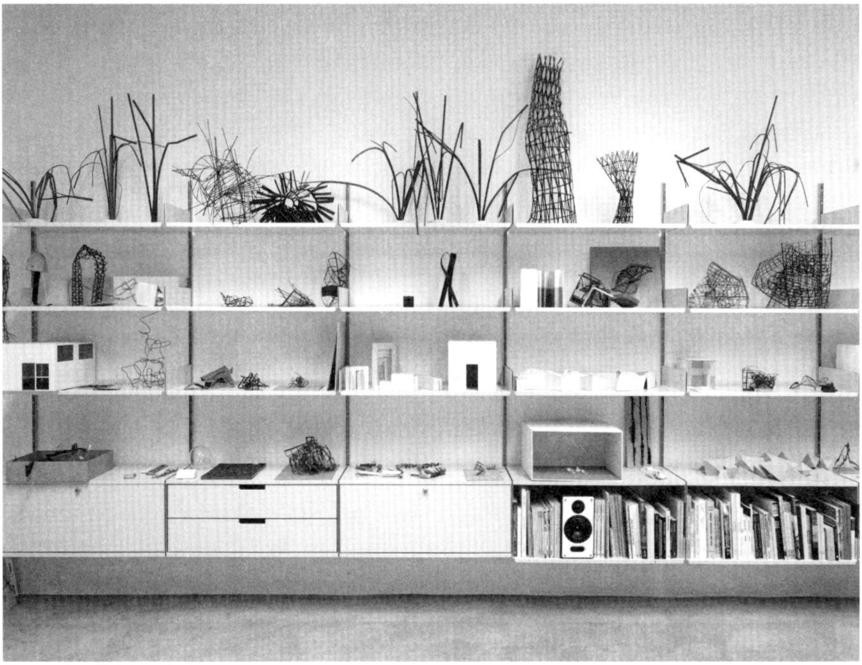

Sosnowska mines the visible elements of architectural modernism; structure, windows and stairs carry the promises of lightness, view and movement but, like everything in the world, these pieces fall to the greater power of nature and entropy. The inevitability of decay and disorder brings about new forms and spaces far away from function. Efficiency becomes useless. Like the ruins celebrated by the nineteenth-century Romantics, her architecture is freed of human requirements and at one with nature. But Sosnowska is not interested in antiquity. Her ruins are all around us today, and in constant flux. The last century saw destruction and reconstruction at scales and speeds previously unknown. Now the utopian promises of postwar reconstruction (in the name of the welfare state in the West or socialism in the East) are themselves being destroyed, replaced by the grabbing hand of global capital dressed up as shiny new developments. Postwar optimism turns into the dust and rubble it once replaced, this time caught in knots of reinforcement. Sosnowska captures these fleeting moments in thin metal wires anchored in plaster clumps, bent into entangled nests.

Steel is the material of modernity, or modernism to be more precise. Concrete and glass might claim the role, but they have existed for far longer, since antiquity. It is steel that made them dance to the twentieth-century beat. And the discovery that steel and concrete share the same thermal expansion coefficient transformed the twentieth century. If you encase bars of steel, which is excellent in tension, in concrete, which is excellent in compression, you produce reinforced concrete, the wonder compound material that emancipated the world. Together they act in sublime harmony for housing, industry or infrastructure. Separated they fall in a knotted mess of wire and rubble, aggressively opposing any kind of future reuse. It would take another century to understand that this was one of the most carbon-emitting marriages ever, and we are still far from reforming it.

Sosnowska creates fragments of these now ubiquitous mineral-ferrous knots. Composed somewhere between architectural wreck and organic growth, these pieces do not comply with the modelmaker's scalpel and steel edge. Springy and disorderly like their real-world counterparts, the modelmaker tries to hold them still. Out comes the hot glue gun. Crude but instant, it will hold the wire in place with a blob of molten plastic. The model takes a turn. Plaster and clay are both column and root ball. Wire remains metallic.

Across shelves and tables the story emerges. Habitable interior installations disappear, leaving traces of human measure in stairs no one will climb and windows no one will open. Once those are gone,

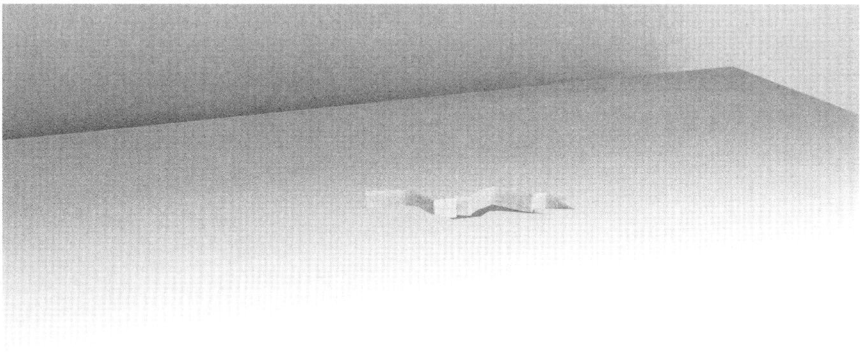

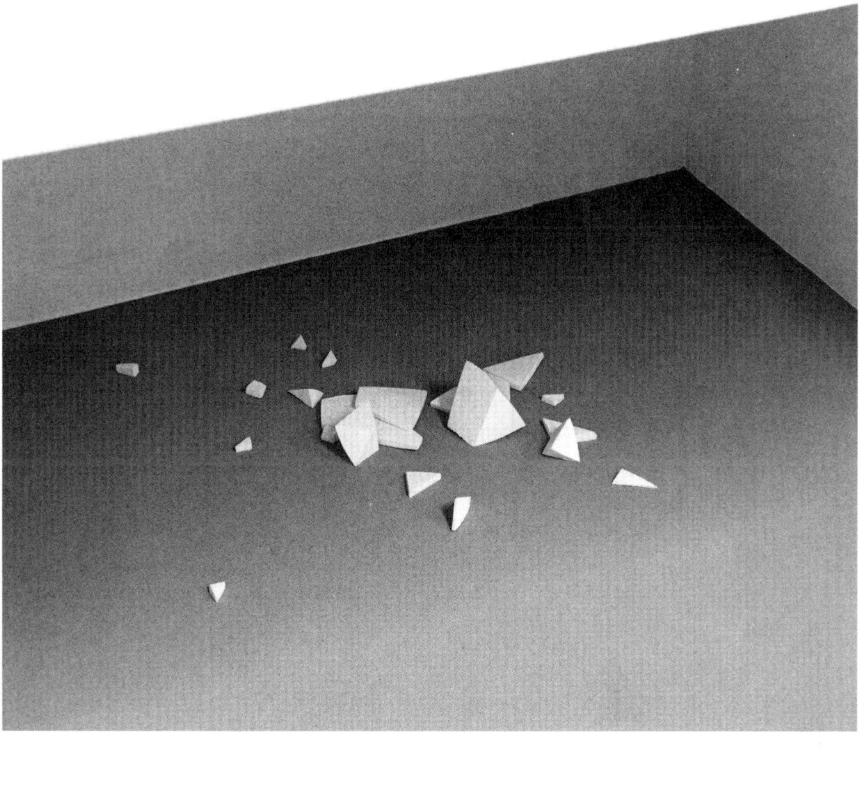

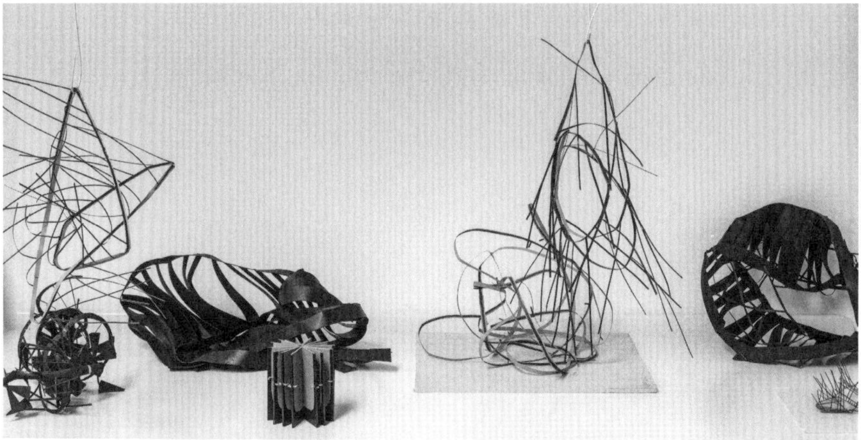

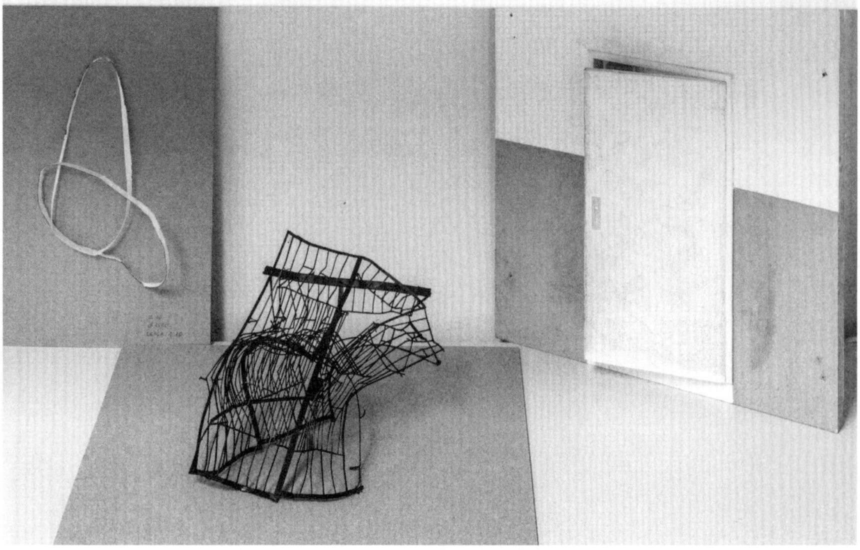

dust and rubble ferociously hold together in tangled steel we were never meant to see. No one will ever see all of these works in one place, not even the artist. Time, space and scale keep things apart. In the studio, and in this exhibition, the models create a meta-work, a world where materials transmit form between objects. What came into being as an intent, an idea in a small artefact, becomes the memory of an artwork far away and a word in a longer story. Together, these ribbons of card create a realm where the weight of the world is transformed by the artist's fingertips, light and free from the burden of human affairs.

PART II
This is Not a Pipe

Please don't tear this page even though it would make my task a whole lot easier. I could rely on the materiality of the paper held in your hand to communicate something that I cannot say in words. I could end the piece by asking you to tear a narrow strip off the bottom of the page and feel or see how the paper would naturally curl, how the edges of fibres behave – feathered and irregular in one direction, neat in the other. Tearing paper is an action of failure; an unsatisfactory draft, an unwelcome message or a secret to be destroyed. It is easy, decisive and quick. But why tear a steel pipe? For starters, it is not torn but cut (probably by an oxy-acetylene flame) and bent, then deliberately twisted over a form to appear as if it were torn even if the forces involved in making *Pipe* (2016) are unrecognisable to the fingertips that roll, fold and tear paper at will, without the need of a guiding eye.

Before working (predominantly) with steel, Sosnowska had for a long time photographed the deep social and political structures embodied in modernism, especially in the Soviet-era modernism of Warsaw and Eastern Europe. With a roving eye for urban photography, she has documented the abstract and rational lines of repeating structures of the modern city, teasing from them both utopian and authoritarian desires. Her images capture the everyday life of modernist planning and design. Grids, prefabrication, open space overlaid with the patina of age and decay; the cold reality of snow and sky that gleams brighter and whiter than the faded structures of industrial socialist society. Steel was not the subject yet was always present somewhere in the scene – proof of the modern. And Sosnowska's images testify to another icon of modernity: the flâneur, drifting across the city collecting small details *par hasard*. The images are not dated but record the end of something, so I would guess they span a couple of decades from the early 1990s. No route is discernible, nor is a predominant subject, material or typology. Interiors are equal to urban wastelands or sunsets. Maybe it is about retaining mementos of a world quickly disappearing under the greedy hand of post-socialist liberal capital, but the project is not that rigorous. It is as if she is searching for something invisible or at least not noticed by a distracted eye, perhaps the thin line of fissure or breakage where the promise of modernity turns to pathos. It is a doomed project because, while it is all around, it cannot be photographed.

But Sosnowska is not looking for images. They are simply *aide-mémoires* along a more embodied quest to give material reality to this invisible

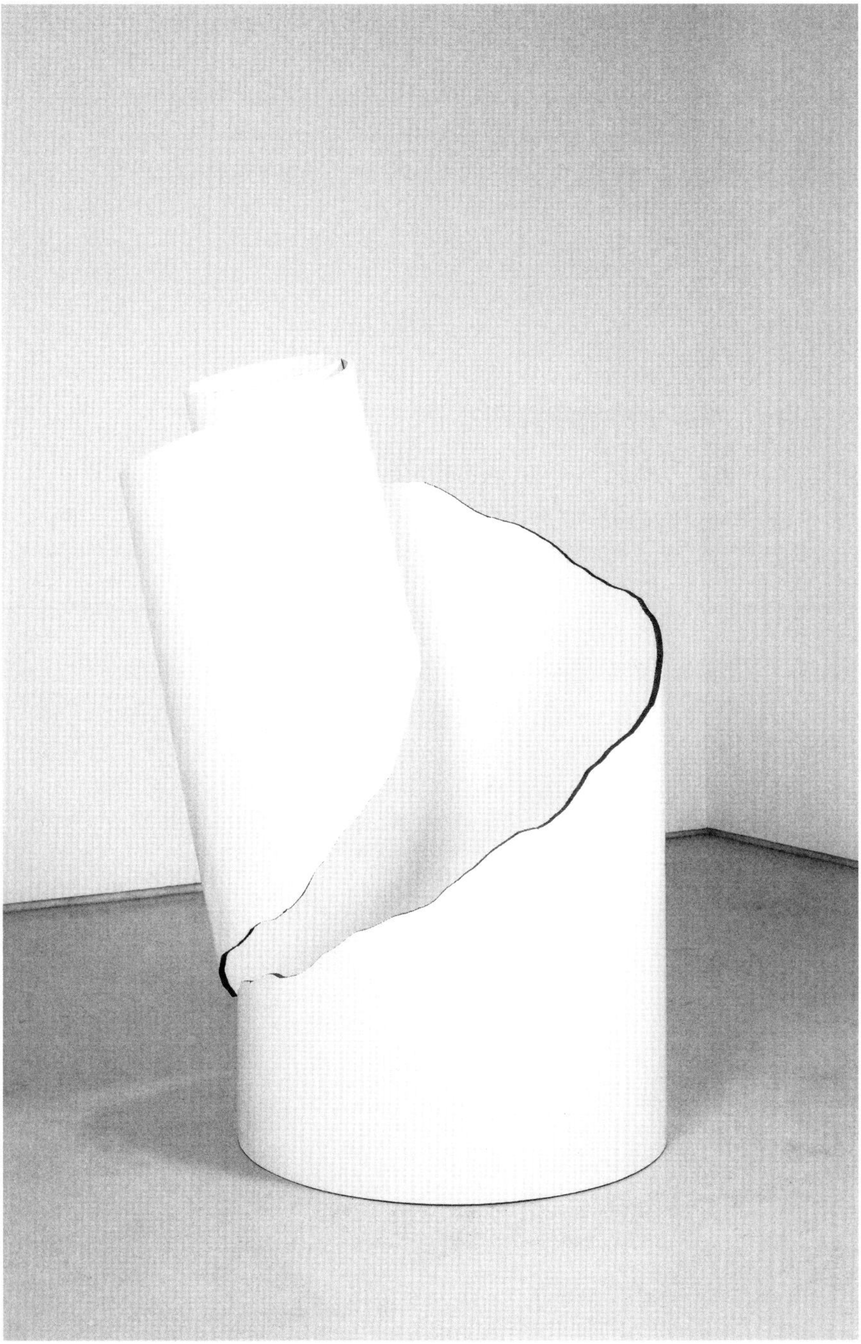

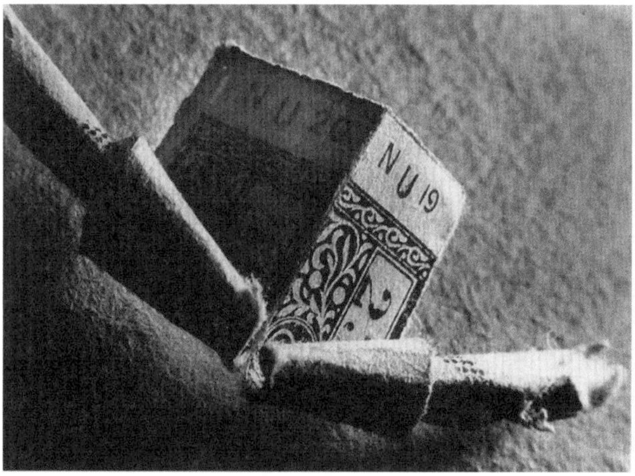
NU 19

process; modernity's troubled journey from promise to disappointment, of progress and resignation. She makes a sculpture by subjecting structure to unreasonable force. Metaphor turned physical. Her structures oscillate between iconic and authored objects and anonymous infrastructure. But steel is the recurring, although not exclusive, material. Temporal specificity (in other words, the twentieth century) combined with malleability gives steel the pass key to unlock the gate that connects success with failure, abstraction with figuration.

Modernist building structure crunched like a car after a crash. A steel spiral stair failing with the melancholic grace of wilting autumn leaves. Mies van der Rohe's pioneering curtain wall facade at Lake Shore Drive rolled up like an old newspaper. And Moscow's Shukhov Tower rudely folded and crushed to fit the museum foyer. It is one of the strange pleasures of Sosnowska's works that one can experience the plastic distortion that is usually associated with failure without losing the epic idea(l)s of their conception. Georges Perec, another scholar of the everyday, asked why trains are only visible when they derail. Why do we need failure to make reality visible?

Modernity provides Sosnowska with a spectrum of objects for transformation. There are the famous works by engineers and architects – like Mies van der Rohe or Shukhov – then there are the anonymous elements of architecture that furnish our environment: stairs, handrails and windows that are often as carefully designed and made in relation to the body. These elements are fundamental to supporting life and movement through space. They are designed not to fail. Sosnowska's works project an alternative fate.

Then there is *Pipe*, which is in many respects a departure. The constructed steel elements shared with other architectural works are of a fundamentally different category. Physically, *Pipe* is a single continuous piece of material. Culturally, a steel pipe was never made to be seen or touched. It is the opposite of the refined rhetoric of modernism. Pipes originate out of site, below ground in infrastructure, possibly real engines of modernity. Whether in a wire, pipe or rail, modernity expresses itself in vectors and movement. Electricity, gas, oil, water, sewage, people and goods moved around further, faster, in greater quantity than ever before. There lies the promise. To tear a pipe is to break the flow.

The architectural pieces evoke a benign nostalgia for mid-twentieth-century optimism, faded on both sides of the Iron Curtain. *Pipe* is altogether more contemporary and violent in its making and meaning. It suggests extraction, fossil fuel, energy, power. Although made five years before Putin's invasion of Ukraine, *Pipe* appears today like a weapon of our times. It speaks of climate crisis, Nord Stream and all the lopsided and expedient geopolitical deals that threaten peace. It is an infrastructure that distributes power, influence and wealth as much as it supplies energy and removes waste. It is the kind of pipe that crosses continents to carry precious resources to sustain cities, economies, political structure and military might. The steel pipe used by Sosnowska – approximately one metre in diameter and one centimetre thick (observed not measured) – is an involuntary monument. Yet here, cut and rolled, painted a luminous white that accentuates the thin darkness of the tear, it stands light and fragile. From one angle it even tilts and spirals, slightly reminiscent of Tatlin's Tower.

Pipe is like a model in reverse. While Sosnowska's delicate models of her architectural works approximate steel structure with paper, *Pipe* simulates the behaviour of card torn and rolled by the artist's hand in steel. The weight, thickness and power of the steel pipe is neutralised. It is not a pipe. No traces of forklifts, oxy-acetylene flame, chains, levers and ratchets. No resources to move. Just a tear and roll, like Brassaï's bus ticket deep inside his pocket.

First published as 'Hanging by a Paperclip', in *Monika Sosnowska: Models*, edited by Martin Waldmeier and Nina Zimmer, Verlag für moderne Kunst, Vienna, 2023; and 'The Monika Papers Part 2: This is Not a Pipe', Roberts Institute of Art, 2023, www.therobertsinstituteofart.com/programme/projects/collection-study-monika-sosnowska

Cutting Corners

A photograph shows two men holding spade-like tools, their cutting edges against a red-earth escarpment. One is raised into the air, about to be thrust downwards, while the blade of the other is already two feet below the ground. The tools belong to a broad category of earth-cutting and moving found all over the world. But these are specific, flatter than a European spade or shovel, the steel end curving slightly into a cutting blade. In fact, they appear more like oversized chisels for carving rather than the digging that has resulted in a sharp vertical face of deep-red clay below a fringe of meadow. It is work in progress. At the base, a series of new horizontal incisions about fifty centimetres tall and two metres long have been cut at forty-five degrees into the dry clay, suggesting more earthworks to come. The action of earth-cutting seems as natural to the place as hammering is to the North American carpenter or stone-cutting to the Italian mason – a culture of making and of work tied to the geology and the territory. Rising above the red escarpment, behind the two men, a prow of brickwork divides the sky as if it has been cut from the very same chisel at work below. It is the leading corner of a new building, a clubhouse and community hall for a football field that is now being carved and levelled from the gently sloping landscape. The image contains the whole project: past, present and future.

The process of earthworks and building appear as one. Forms carved in the ground echo the form built above them. Of course, soon after this picture is taken the football field will be flat and the escarpment neatly terraced up to the building. But the building will retain a powerful resonance of previous events, signifying the arrival of the beautiful game.

The figures in the landscape are part of a series of precisely and practically honed architectural operations. The Centre d'Education FC Advan comprises three buildings and a freshwater well, all set around a football field that forms a great landscape structure. As host to the local football team and schoolchildren, the centre is a community space for sports and education in Ambanja, northern Madagascar. The project was initiated and funded by Viktor Bänziger, owner of El Lokal cultural bar in Zurich, who, seduced by the music and musicians from Madagascar performing in his venue, set off to discover the country. Since his love for music is matched only by his love of football, Bänziger's journey to Madagascar rather unsurprisingly led to the creation of a place for sport and education.

The Centre d'Education FC Advan is literally made from the ground on which it stands, but it is also an exchange between continents. Successful building projects often involve a combination of sustained purpose to achieve a goal with coincidence that turns effort into opportunity. When Bänziger needed someone to design the buildings, he knew not only an architect with a kindred spirit for the social aims of the project but also one of the rare contemporary practitioners with a profound understanding of brick. Several years before, during her architectural studies at ETH Zurich, Nele Dechmann had undertaken research on the monolithic brick Church of St Bride (Gillespie, Kidd & Coia, East Kilbride, Scotland, 1957), relatively unknown in continental Europe. Heavy, earthy, with very occasional delicate turns – here was an architecture as ancient as it was modern, as formally abstract as it was pragmatic. The study of this unsung corner of architectural history was, for Dechmann, the beginning of an architectural journey into the contemporary use of traditional materials. She replayed it in her wonderful library in Köpenick, Berlin (2008), which reinterpreted the deep brick diaphragm walls of the church for circulation and small study chambers around the main halls.

So it was only natural that the red clay that defines the landscape and traditional brick architecture of the northern highlands of Madagascar would be the means and ends of the community buildings for the football club. Images from the site and surrounding villages are marked by vivid red-clay paths that draw lines across the landscape and in the simple rectangular volumes of local buildings. Once fired, the red clay emerges lighter, but its deep colour often returns when the houses are rendered in the unfired material. The actions of cutting, digging, forming and firing are fundamental to any architectural culture capable of transforming its ground into structure and space, yet an architectural language always bears unique characteristics of scale, bond and texture. Scale is closely tied to the body and the hand. Each brick is stacked according to bond patterns for strength and sculptural effect. Material and structural efficiency has brought brick into partnership with structural framing – usually, but not always, in reinforced concrete. But brickwork cannot be understood as purely image. Dechmann started with her own visit to Madagascar, studying not only the buildings but the entire process from earth to house, from geology to community.

The three buildings reflect much of what she experienced and documented on site. They bear a strong relationship to the village architecture, but they are also other. The traditions, economies and technologies that determine architectural design are all at play but transformed just enough for a slight abstraction, turning building into a new architecture. Aligned with the pitch's centre line is the clubhouse classroom, the largest of the three buildings. The corners of the rectangular plan are cut off at forty-five degrees, leaving the oversailing timber pitched roof. In one simple operation, the local type reveals a series of spatial and formal inventions without rhetoric or unnecessary expense. For the users, the corners create four external spaces outside the double-height hall overlooking the pitch, sheltered from the blistering sun. The plan playfully embodies the ninety- and forty-five-degree angles without discomfort. In the landscape, a new form emerges from familiar origins. Cutting the corners creates a striking vertical line that runs up the centre, extending the tallest dimension of the building to the apex of the roof. The leading edge divides the sunlight into even finer geometries of brightness and shade. It is as if the halfway line of the football pitch has been extended right up to the heavens – the symmetry of the game raised into architecture.

The free overhanging corners of the roof are propped up by tall brick columns; stout at the base and narrowing as they rise to pick up the load. This is a pragmatic and efficient use of material but also a matter of form and lightness. Terracotta tiles with half-round ends, also made from the red clay, cover the roofs of the two primary buildings; the third is thatched. The process and project are full of space and form, not in some aloof manner of distant theory but the product of human action and exchange: action on the part of the architect that gives agency to all the physical and organisational processes by people on the ground. Dechmann has described the whole project as an assembly of simple parts between Zurich and Ambanja, carefully and concisely laid out in three-dimensional line drawings like those for a model aeroplane. Starting with the single unit of brick, the bonding patterns are arranged and geometries clearly laid out with small details providing accents for significant moments.

From afar, the buildings have something of a temple about them. Familiar but strange, perhaps like the monumentality of the brick kilns that Dechmann documented? No, lighter: more like the abstract geometry of a football pitch, used in the same way all over the world yet leaving no two games alike. Close up, a more tactile dimension is revealed. Two modest areas of brickwork laid obliquely produce a field of small shadows around the entrance, recalling the brick corbels over the entrance to St Bride's – small gestures where the makers will welcome the users in a pattern of light and shadow. And to finish it all, the exposed concrete frame – painted in the same pink as the window frames – blends contrasting materials while adding a touch of millennial style.

The men have finished their work. The tools have been put away. The pitch is level and neatly terraced up to the slope. The buildings stand in material union with the ground, geometry aligned with the game. Boys and girls in vertically striped blue-and-yellow kit marked 'El Lokal' take the crucial corner.

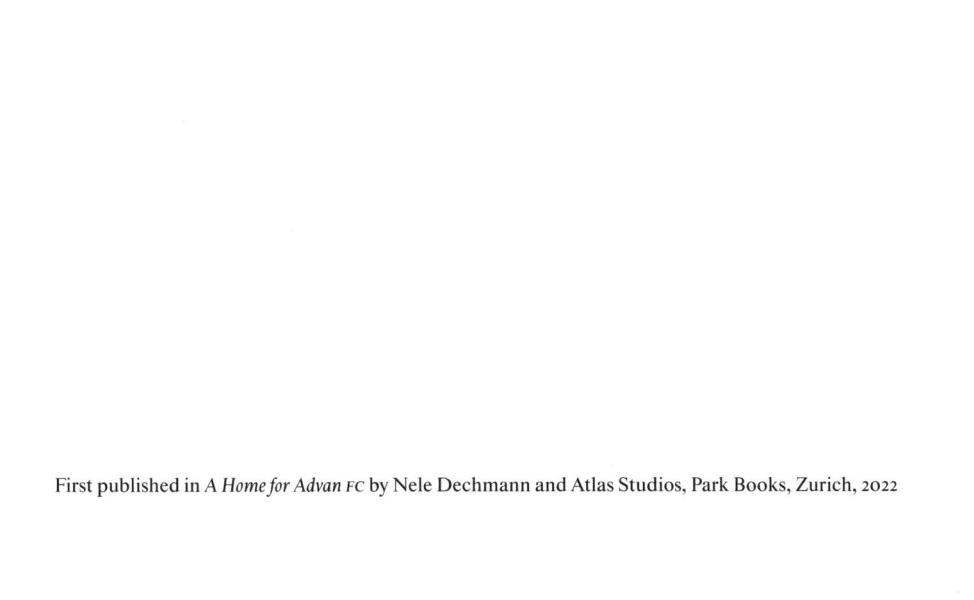

First published in *A Home for Advan* FC by Nele Dechmann and Atlas Studios, Park Books, Zurich, 2022

Tolerance

Too many people have talked about how profoundly the production of architecture has changed in the wake of the digital revolution. Far fewer have noted how architecture has resisted the seductive flourishes of digital production and maintained a dogged continuity with social and historical space. Bricks remain bricky even when laid by a robot. Timber remains fibrous despite the scorched traces of the laser cutter. These remain the rare marriages of new technologies with ancient tectonics, for architecture continues to evolve within the present, dragging a past into the future full of conflicted meanings and associations.

Occasionally architecture is also revolutionary, rupturing with the past to establish the unencumbered new. Paper architecture has long been a byword for the avant-garde, for the unbuilt as much as unbuildable architectural rhetoric. Yet even in revolution, the representation of architecture uses the same abstract notation of orthographic plans, sections and elevations established during the Renaissance. As with all architectural (r)evolutions, the primary battleground since that time has been in drawings and, dare I say it, on paper. The architectural drawing sits ambiguously between revolution and tradition.

The past three centuries have seen a complete transformation in industrial production and society. In the last twenty years, communication has done the same. Despite these changes, the architectural drawing – the plan – has endured: architects still examine the plan to understand its underlying spatial and conceptual ideas. This survival places the plan in the realm of a quasi-language rather than professional technique, a system possessing its own rules and codes, unlinked to the phenomena it represents. In this case, the common language that bridges the architectural imagination with a constructed reality lies in the conventions of the plan. Like musical notation, the architectural drawing is composed and read by the initiated, a semi-open code of ideas and instructions specifying exact execution or inviting interpretation. It is a means of creation, production, reproduction, execution and one of very few means of production to endure despite more than five centuries of changes in culture and technique – from steel point and quill to graphite, mechanical ink pens and finally CAD, which replaced the hand in the closing decade of the twentieth century. Augmented realities and AI now put it all into question.

The first time I entered an architectural office was in 1989 for a summer job I had taken before starting architecture school. The office of around forty people was quiet and busy with designers either standing or sitting on tall stools and hunching over drawing boards arranged at assorted angles to suit their users. My first task was to change fire exits on a plan from single doors to double doors. A simple if rather banal task for a young would-be architect. I was shown to my board and handed my first Rotring pen, scale ruler, blue clutch pencil and, crucially, a small packet of razor blades to erase the offending doors scattered across the A0 tracing paper drawing.

Like all skills required of a good draftsman or woman, scraping away a very thin layer of ink without damaging the paper requires practice. I clumsily gouged away more paper than ink with the razor and eventually cut through my finger. The rest of the day was occupied with removing dried blood from the complex field of fine black lines that formed the primary ground-floor plan, known as the general arrangement drawing, or GA for short. Needless to say, I developed the art of erasure ahead of the full range of drafting skills, but for the record, in time, those also improved.

Over the following five years, both at architecture school and in offices, we would draw for several hours a day, gaining speed and precision alongside an awareness of the nuances of architectural drawings. Ink on trace was the modus operandi of a British practice, but occasionally one would use film, a heavy-duty translucent plastic sheet that looks like tracing paper but behaves in a completely different way. Film is tough stuff. It was used for long-term drawing that would be updated over years – say, the ground plan of a major building. But film does not absorb ink, it stays liquid on the surface for what seems like an eternity when facing a deadline, and it can be erased with a special rubber (or eraser, probably electric, for our American colleagues). At the other end of the scale, in smaller offices, one would use pencil on detail paper, thin and soft, a cousin of tissue paper favoured for wrapping luxury goods. With pencil and detail paper (mounted over a sheet of cartridge paper backing to soften the stroke), the work of the draftsman felt more personal, more subtle. One could do the whole process with a single tool. Light construction lines ghosting out the drawing followed by a firmer stroke especially at the start and end of each line while rotating the mechanical to keep the point sharp. With pencil, not only was drawing faster, but the sheet of paper acquired a texture and reflected the hand of the author more directly. One could discern the work of the manic, rushed architect chasing construction site deadlines from the subtle marks left by the reflective practitioner. These were the tools of our trade.

It is worth defining what kind of plans we are looking at. In German, the plan refers to all the technical drawings leading to construction, whether horizontal or vertical. In English, the plan refers specifically to a horizontal section while the whole set of construction documents, including plans, sections, elevations and construction details, is commonly referred to as working drawings. Adding the verb 'working' lends a particular kind of technical and ethical purpose. These are not objects of contemplation, of aesthetic quality; they are work and they represent more work to be done. They may be seen as a means to an end and nothing more. But of course this has never been entirely true. The architect has always invested the working drawing with more than pure information and data to share with builders. Either deliberately or inadvertently, the working drawing is laced with conceptual and ethical values that underpin the architecture. The architect's plan combines everything that is common to the language of architecture, its traditions and conventions, with what is personal and unique, like a form of handwriting.

As a student, seeing Peter Zumthor's drawings of Saint Benedict Chapel in Sumvitg, Switzerland (1989), published in a 1990 issue of *Architectural Review*, was particularly memorable for their combination of precision and atmosphere. These were not black lines on white but shades of grey lines on grey background. I had not seen the building (and still haven't to this day), but I believed (and still do) that the qualities of those drawings would be found there, regular but sensual, austere without being cold. Like many of my peers, I had fairly promiscuous architectural taste and studied Frank Gehry's early work with equal enthusiasm. One doesn't need to travel from Switzerland to LA to find the difference between the timber buildings of either architect. Both work predominantly with softwood frames, but their construction traditions and inventions couldn't be further apart, and their working drawing techniques bring out that difference. Although both use pencil, Zumthor's drawings are above all complete works in their own right. The mise-en-page perfectly places the subject on the sheet. Layers of overlapping lines, from barely visible grid lines to the heaviness of elements cut by the imagined section to the regularity of the hatching, speak of patience, resilience. Nothing is left to chance. Tolerance has certainly been considered, but this is dimensional tolerance, technical tolerance where it is required by the material that masks another kind of intolerance. Every element in the architecture has been considered and honed. Mistakes do not form part of Zumthor's architecture. In LA, however, all of Gehry's lines are broadly equivalent, democratic and, above all, quick. The drawing shows what is necessary and no more. There is no time for hatching. This is no meditation over reduction and craftsmanship but instead fast, intuitive riffing on well-known commercial vernacular. The notation and construction are economic, even expedient, the results refreshingly direct. There is plenty of tolerance both dimensionally and also ethically, allowing the carpenter to complete the task according to prevailing rules of commercial construction. Gehry's working drawings are loose and opportunistic. But one shouldn't be deceived into believing that these drawings suggest lesser importance to construction. On the contrary, both architects show a deep knowledge of construction, materials and a wider socio-economic context. Gehry's apparently laconic plans embody the tradition of American timber-framed construction just as profoundly as Zumthor's drawings suggest the craftsmanship for which he and the Swiss are so famous. The drawing is not only a means to an end, it also suggests the means.

'This is how space begins', writes Georges Perec in the opening of *Species of Spaces*, 'signs traced on the blank page', but such direct, unmediated creation is no longer possible. When I finished my studies in 1997, the craft of architectural draftsmanship already seemed about as useful as calligraphy. Today, paper is the final resting place for the line after a life of digital gymnastics. Layers, classes, attributes, NURBS; so many decisions before space can begin. The stroke of the pencil or pen has been replaced by the click of the mouse, the rectangular expanse of the drawing board by the infinite zoom of the screen. And yet the orthographic projection of the plan remains the lingua franca of architecture. The plan is both the thinking and the letting go, the conception and the communication with the maker, taking the architectural imagination into the world line by line. Although it is no longer drawn in the original meaning of the word – that is, by pulling a pencil across a surface – the plan retains a uniquely autonomous position in architecture between the architect and the built architecture. The great conceit of the plan – to imagine the work of architecture sliced horizontally to reveal simultaneously its solids and voids, its surfaces and nodes – is an improbable but powerful abstraction. After the point, the line is the most basic Cartesian form, yet in the context of the plan it is capable of representing a multitude of spatial ideas. The line may signify the physical and the abstract; it may suggest a surface, a gesture like the spread of a trowel or an invisible legal boundary. The line can suggest changes in the states of matter between mass and void or between a liquid and its container. Or the containment might exist in the lines themselves as they come together to make the working drawing, a register of a temporal dimension that encompasses both the pre-existing and the as-yet-unrealised anticipated future. The drawing contains a latent architectural order; densely layered or monolithic, dotted to float above or thickened to suggest the imaginary slice through plaster, steel or concrete.

The plan is the making of the architecture. It is the instrument by which the architect records what is found and proposes what will come. The plan is the means of conception and communication. In the end, the plan is not so much musical notation or handwriting as it is the fingerprints of the architect, both universal and unique. More than the sketch, which communicates intuition and first thoughts, the plan bears the imprint of the whole process through to every decision, whether invented or imposed from the outside. The working drawing contains the sum total of the architect's thinking, time spent, compromises, imagination and skill synthesised and distilled in lines on paper.

First published as 'Lines on Paper' in *Der Bauplan: Werkzeug des Architekten* by Annette Spiro and David Ganzoni (ETH Zurich), Park Books, Zurich, 2013

Blue

Architect's Office, London NW1, Summer 1990

A van delivers boxes of dyelines to the office. More than one hundred A1 line drawings made on tracing paper and copied four times must be sent out to contractors today. They have to be checked and collated into four piles, then folded three times so the bottom right corner showing the drawing number faces out as an A4 sheet. As the youngest in the office it is my job to fold, count and pile. I like the strong smell of ammonia. It feels professional. This is architecture.

Fresh dyelines are crisp blue traces on off-white background, like negatives of the traditional blueprint. The drawing has to be made with ink on thick tracing paper or film to allow light to pass through onto photosensitive diazo paper. The blueish cast across the dyeline varies slightly with each batch, perhaps because of differences in paper thickness or the age of the chemicals. But it doesn't matter, as the freshness will not last long. Old dyelines around the office have yellowed or darkened depending on their age. The sharp lines have faded, too, like old tattoos. Paste-ups of labels or diagrams leave traces of the invisible tape holding them in position.

Folding a dyeline is a skill, more like the complex sequence of folding a map into more than simply halves. The blue cast surface of a dyeline paper creates an extra-dry resistance against the fingertips. The feeling is pleasant at first, as each neat crease emits a little heat into the fingernail doing the folding. Friction soon turns to light abrasion, but the lightheadedness from ammonia eases the task. The blueprint is smell and touch more than it is colour.

Later that summer the first CAD station arrived at the office. I think I have not seen a new dyeline since – at least I have not folded one. Now there is no smell. There are no dyelines. There is no blue.

Openings
Conversations with the Álvaro Siza Archive

Álvaro Siza is deeply interested in hinges. He has told me this himself, but more importantly, you can see it in the working drawings made during the first two decades of his career, from 1954 onwards. Occasionally done in ink but more often in pencil, hundreds of drawings show a slow and deliberate evolution from vernacular elements based in traditional craftsmanship to a specific and personal architectural language expanding into the spatial constellations that have come to define his oeuvre. Not only hinges but also latches, catches, locks and stays form part of the construction of the windows and doors that alongside machined profiles give architecture its use and its language. Although these elements are increasingly homogenised into global products, their origins are specific to climate, wealth and scarcity, taste, technology, geology, trade and politics.

While working on his first project, Four Dwellings in Matosinhos (1954–57), built when he was only twenty-one, Siza discovered the difference between the carpenters from the north and those from the south of Portugal. To lock the hinge in place the northern carpenter inserted dry timber pegs which expanded with moisture absorbed from the atmosphere. At this time Siza was still in architecture school and learning by talking to the craftsmen directly, not only about the few technical details missing from his education but also to develop an understanding of the specificity of building culture. The skills of the carpenter from the north could be traced back to a tradition in boat building; a tradition which by its very nature is also about travel, trade and exchange. Perhaps that seafaring way of life explains the similarities between the vertically sliding sash windows in Porto and London's eighteenth- and nineteenth-century streetscape.

From the late 1950s to the early 1970s Siza's architectural language evolves. Window frames are enlarged and flattened while large planes of hardwood intensify the views outside and the fluidity of spaces within. Gate posts and doors start merging asymmetrically with the wall and into the landscape without losing the craftsman's fingertip knowledge for the natural assembly of materials. These are no longer openings belonging to a taxonomy of building components that Rem Koolhaas would later display in Venice as the elements of architecture, or which Aldo Rossi would symbolise through his analogous reading of the discipline. Siza's openings, like his celebrated freehand sketches, are fluid. As the latch releases the door in the asymmetric gate of the Rocha Ribeiro House (1962), the threshold reveals a microcosm of the whole residence. The gate announces the movement and stillness that define the house and its landscape. The window frame becomes a shutter which in turn becomes a bench. Inside, the same elements become an exaggerated skirting leading through space that suddenly turns vertical to mark a corner light. Occasionally multiple planes of dark timber fuse into a single view only to be disaggregated into the landscape one step later.

This fragmented sequence of openings is more singular in the Lordelo do Ouro Cooperative (1960-70). One continuous ribbon of hardwood windows folds around the faceted concrete base, defining the external area as something between working yard and civic space, before then leading inside, guiding a public route through the building. Sadly, today much of this intricate articulation of inside and outside can only be imagined from Siza's working drawings, as most of it has been replaced with aluminium glazing patched with roofing felt flashings. And yet Siza's empathy for the users of his buildings remains visible in a humble servicing cupboard and single stockroom door, both of which have

escaped the expedient refurbishment. Here again, he uses traditional carpentry to create a single opening of enormous hardwood sections forty centimetres wide by six centimetres thick. These were the last days of abundant African hardwoods and before colonial legacies were culturally and materially challenged. The drawings at 1:100, 1:20 and full-size describe how thicknesses and the weight of timber openings not only match the concrete of the superstructure above, but even appear to support it. Plans, sections and schematic three-dimensional sketches fit together just as every piece of wood is precisely placed into recesses cast in concrete.

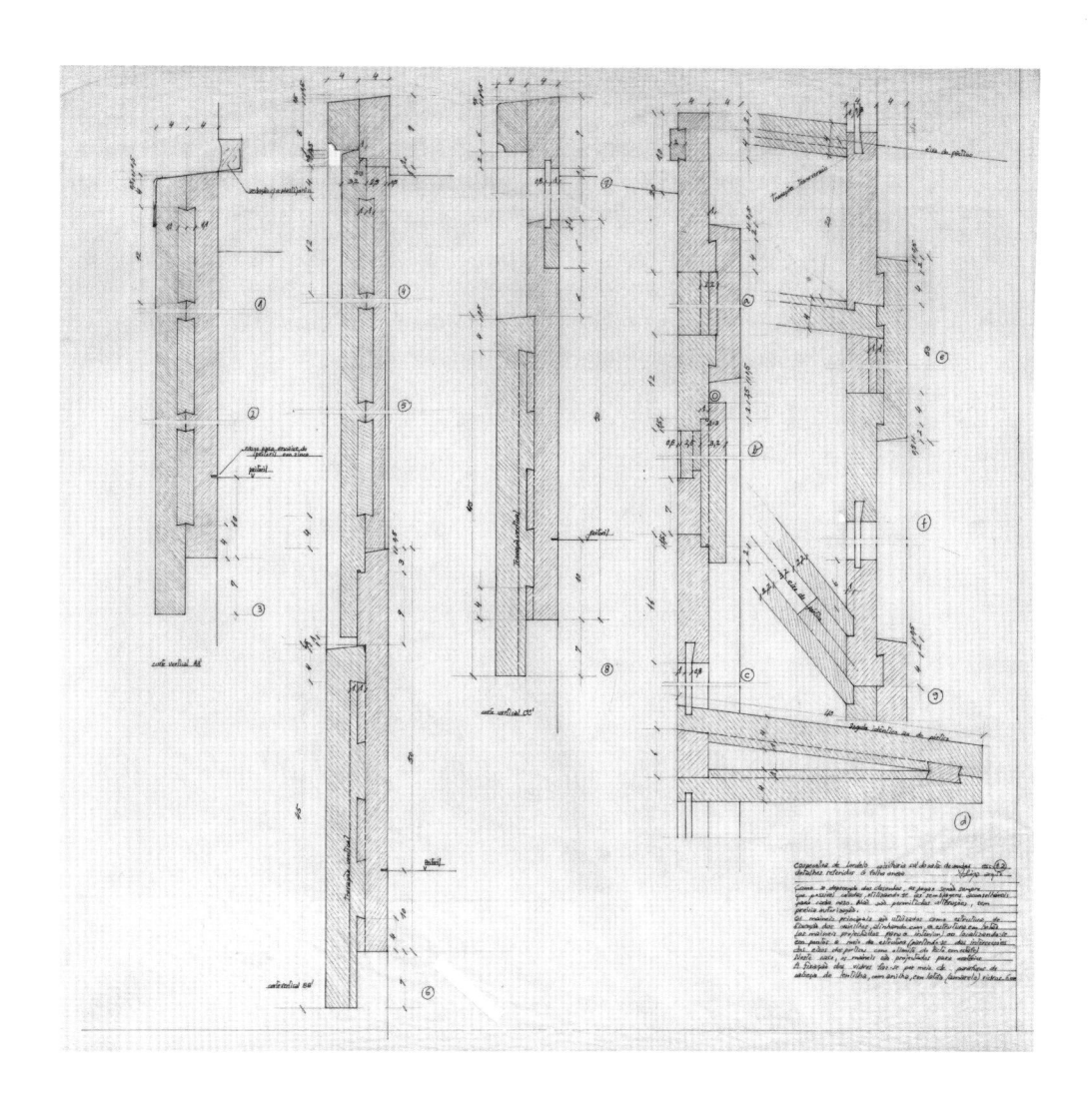

Opposite and overleaf: Lordelo do Ouro Cooperative, Porto, Portugal, 1960–63
Above: South-facing carpentry details of shopping area, undated

A great deal has already been said about the artfulness of Siza's sketches and his poetic imagination. They confirm his humanity as well as his politics and social engagement. If we cannot experience all of his buildings directly we can understand his architecture from the thousands of sketches which flow incessantly from his pen. In the foreground a foot or left hand holding a cigarette situates him within the scene. Occasionally an angel flies overhead. For speed or for emphasis, a line arcs over the space populated with human action in direct encounter with architectural reflections and search. The hand that draws so lyrically is the same as the one that made the working drawings; the full-scale detail and the landscape in which he is working are never far apart. They explore the whole and the fragment and contain the memory of conversations (with carpenters, clients, residents). Today artistry has higher cultural capital than professionalism, which explains the number of exhibitions and books dedicated to sketches of all types. Working drawings are the product of a professionalism to which Siza has unfailingly dedicated his career but is rarely credited. Evidence of graft and grind, long hours and effort dilute the myth of creation so highly prized today. His construction drawings reflect his ethical and political constitution to serve society professionally. They are the place where the architecture is conceived, developed, tested, corrected and refined in an iterative process rarely visible in the final work. Often stained by late-night coffees and cigarettes, these drawings then become the communication with those builders and craftsmen from whom the architect has learned so much.

Openings: Conversations with the Álvaro Siza Archive

The two decades that follow Four Dwellings in Matosinhos align multiple phases in Siza's own career with external political events. Like many young architects, he was producing the drawings himself. Both the private houses around Porto and the small to medium-sized public buildings allowed, even demanded, intimacy and direct engagement with the production of drawings. In the 1950s and 1960s, Portugal's building industry lagged behind other European countries. But what it lacked in terms of modern building systems, it made up for in available materials from African colonies and traditional skills. Siza found in those conditions an evolutionary way of working, based on tradition. One comes across many photographs of Siza on construction sites. Time moved slower then, construction was pliable and responsive to contingencies. Such conditions allowed the architect to continuously refine what was drawn as work progressed. One could develop a contemporary language slowly, starting with local traditions before abstracting and inventing a way into their own times and beyond. For Siza, this period of development prepared him for a life in architecture even if everything changed dramatically after the revolution of 1974. Houses became housing and openings became sparer. Limited public sector budgets and a postcolonial politics could no longer support the lavish material and high craftsmanship of those early projects. But even in this new period of reduced architectural expression, the embodied knowledge in those buildings, those traditions, those drawings remains a defining feature of Siza's architecture.

Once you know a little about Siza's work, it becomes easy to recognise – even across his six-decade career. There are the recurring motifs: the landscape-like spatial fluidity articulated in a limited material palette – white stucco with timber in the early work, later replaced by stone linings and bases. Openings are unique to each project yet the language is recognisable, like handwriting which evolves over a lifetime but always remains true to its owner. A Siza sketch is equally familiar. His construction drawings reveal a similar consistency, mainly in the refined layering of light pencil as it constructs lines, gradually gaining weight as the section of materials is evenly hatched, ready for the construction. Confirmation of Siza's hand may be found in a signature at the bottom right corner or notes and dimensions precisely inscribed to finalise the assembly. They follow the conventions of architectural draftsmanship, but the drawing is undeniably Siza's.

In the irregular glass crescent of the Beires House (1972–76) Siza makes a virtuoso performance of flowing space and draftsman's line. The house is defined by a solid, two-storey, L-shaped wall from which

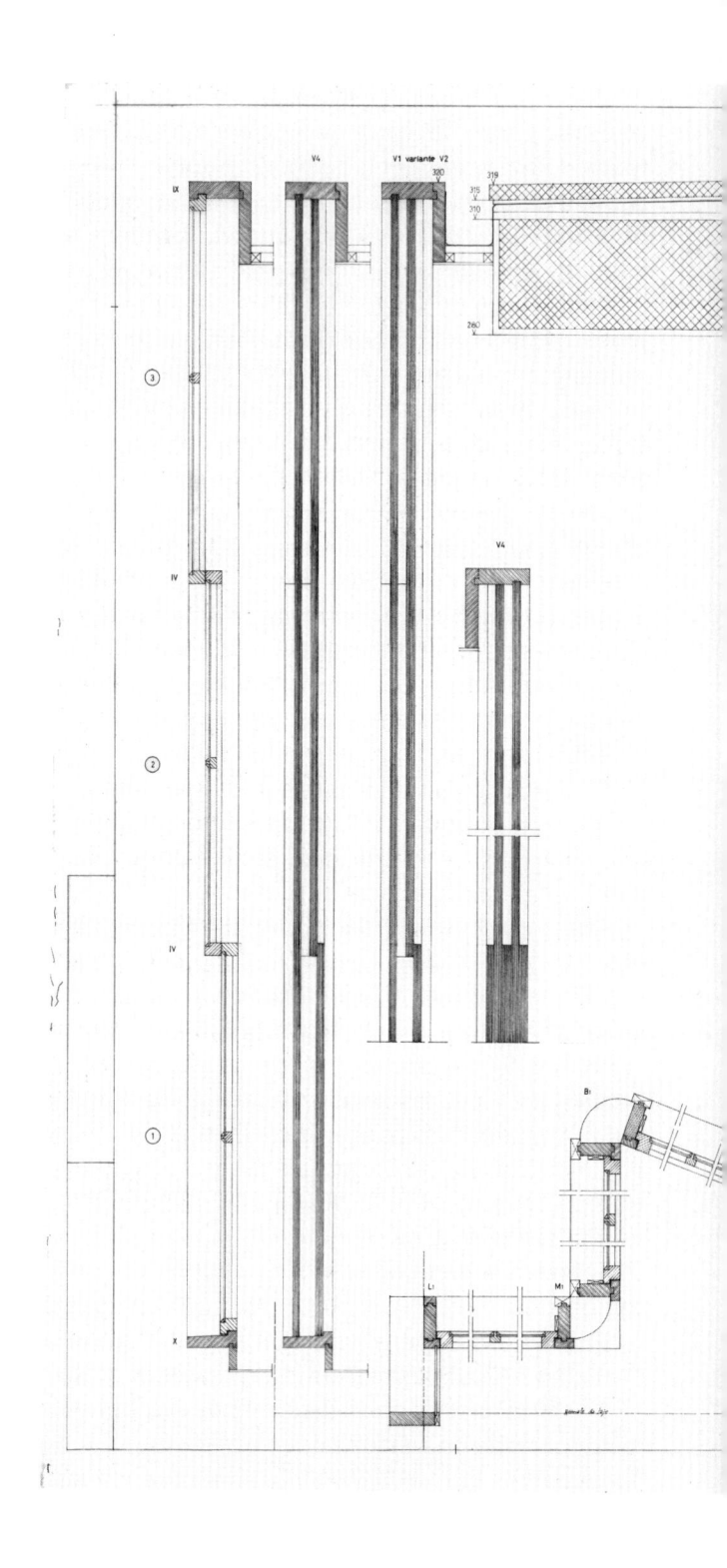

Carlos Beires House, Póvoa de Varzim, Portugal, 1973–79. Technical project: carpentry details of first-floor window, undated

V4 - fixa / sobe / porta

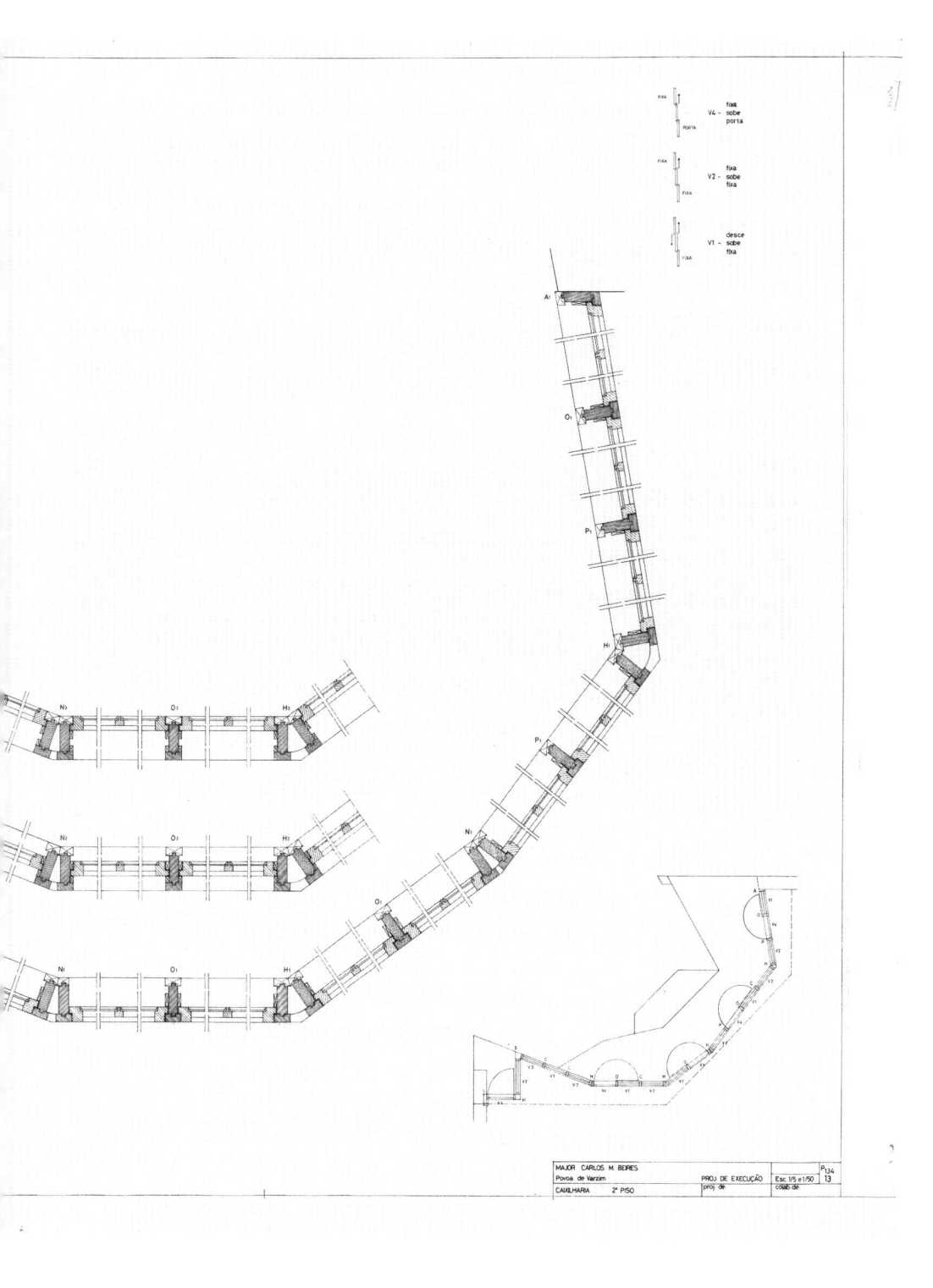

V2 - fixa / sobe / fixa

V1 - desce / sobe / fixa

MAJOR CARLOS M. BEIRES			P 134
Povoa de Varzim	PROJ DE EXECUÇÃO	Esc. 1/5 e 1/50	13
CAIXILHARIA 2º PISO	proj de	colab de	

undulating screens of timber and glass dramatically crack open the interior to the outside world. The working drawings appear organic, like an Aalto plan or vase. But within the flowing forms, you find the carpenter's knowledge of twenty years earlier. With the help of a lightly sketched human figure standing beside the section, a traditional sash window emerges as the repeating element. That ancient window with layers of glass and timber sliding over one another for light, air or shade, shared by so many cities by the sea, is drawn over and over until Siza has made it new again and opened it to the horizon.

Carlos Beires House, Póvoa de Varzim, Portugal, 1973-79

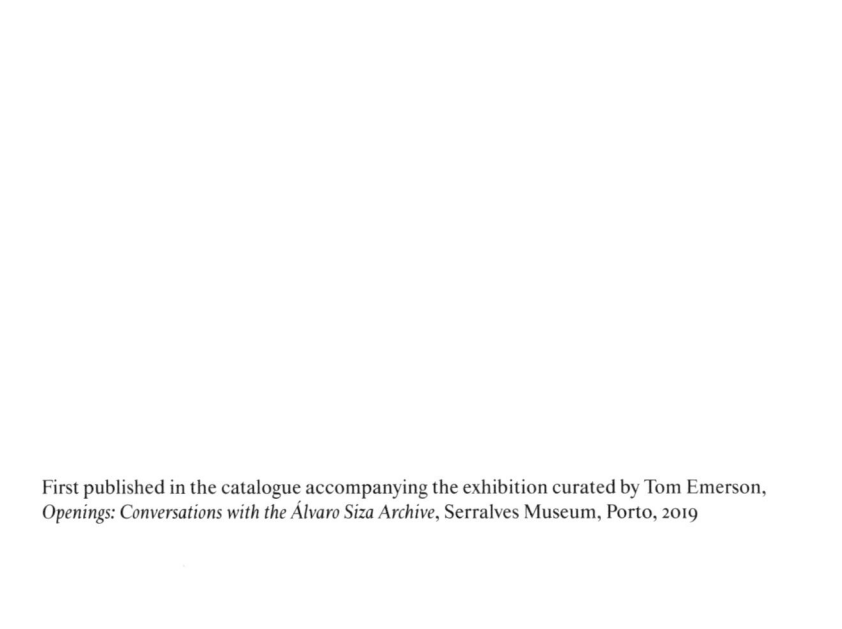

First published in the catalogue accompanying the exhibition curated by Tom Emerson,
Openings: Conversations with the Álvaro Siza Archive, Serralves Museum, Porto, 2019

From *Lieux* to Life...

Googling 11 Rue Simon-Crubellier, Paris, produces a great crop of entries over several screen pages. Selecting 'maps' generates a red pin in the seventeenth arrondissement attributed to Gaspard Winckler, painter and decorator, which is populated with five-star reviews, even if one reviewer remarks that Winckler himself is rather 'puzzling'. Not a bad result for an imaginary place. 11 Rue Simon-Crubellier is the fictional address of the apartment building at the centre of Georges Perec's great urban and architectural novel *Life A User's Manual* (1978), and Gaspard Winckler is the resident puzzle maker fiendishly trying to outdo Bartlebooth's project of five hundred seascape jigsaw puzzles. In 1996, when I wrote the first version of this piece as my graduate dissertation, *Spaces in Words: The Treatment of Space in the Writing of Georges Perec*, an internet search was a matter for the university computer department which in all probability would have revealed few maps, real or imaginary, and even less about Perec. In 2002, for a Perec-themed double issue of AA *Files*, I returned to Bartlebooth and his neighbours to produce a shorter version of the dissertation. By then, Google had found its place in the world but there was not yet the dizzying conflation of real, false and imaginary material that inundates our consciousness today. *Life A User's Manual* was well established as a literary classic and Perec's *Species of Spaces*, written earlier, in 1974, but only translated in 1997, was quickly becoming essential reading in architectural circles beyond France.

Lieux did exist in parts in some far corners of experimental literary journals available through inter-library loans while other fragments had been published in elegant slim volumes such as *Tentative d'épuisement d'un lieu parisien* (1975). But most importantly, it was in *Species of Spaces* that Perec announced both *Life A User's Manual* as a project to come, and *Lieux* as a work in progress.

> Space melts like sand running through one's fingers. Time bears it away and leaves me only shapeless shreds:
> To write: to try meticulously to retain something, to cause something to survive: to wrest some precise scraps from the void as it grows, to leave somewhere a furrow, a trace, a mark or a few signs.[1]

In 1969 Georges Perec set out to record the places of Paris that were meaningful to his life. He devised a highly structured system of describing ordinary places that produced texts in time capsules as well as a natural real-time autobiography. He called the project *Lieux*. Over twelve years, Perec wrote about twelve places, each with a strong personal resonance in his own life. Each place was described twice – once when visited in person, and once more from memory. The project united three of Perec's principal concerns: the sociology of everyday spaces, autobiography and experimental poetics. The simultaneous descriptions permitted and forced him to go into the city's spaces, looking, seeing, observing and writing, all within the same act. Both place and Perec were physically present on each occasion, giving him the opportunity, through slow and repeated immersion, to interrogate the space through description, noting everything. When in 1975 Perec eventually renounced the project, it in no way signalled a failure but instead marked a kind of renaissance of his own evolution as a writer. He immediately began work on *Life A User's Manual*, a project that had been slowly maturing for years[2] and which served as a fictional mirror image of *Lieux*. Despite his long-standing commitment to real observation and description, Perec was increasingly looking towards the freedoms offered by fiction,[3] albeit under the dizzying complexity of linguistic, mathematical constraints. He was turning inward, shifting from the recollection of a single life across the spaces of the city to the representation of the world through the interior world of a single building.

The publication of *Species of Spaces* in 1974 marked the beginning of Perec's explicit concern with seeing and describing spaces and things, but as *Lieux* suggests, he had been developing his attitudes towards an 'anthropology of everyday life' for some time.[4] The spatial structure of events and their inhabitants had been a key part of his fiction since the earliest novels of the mid-1960s. Characters in his writings are often built from the world that surrounds them. Frequently that world is Paris. In Perec's first novel, *Things* (1965), the accumulation and display of objects in the city comes to define the material yet futile desires of Jérôme and Sylvie, a young couple who, along with their environment, serve as the subjects of a quasi-scientific sociological study of the pitfalls of consumer society; they are a couple who define themselves through things. The narrative progresses flatly, describing the objects Jérôme and Sylvie possess and those they desire, differentiating the two characters by the use of present tense or the conditional. In such works, Perec concentrates on what is usually ignored or taken for granted, the mundane details of everyday life: gestures involved in parking a car or the manner in which people hold their newspapers. A similar descriptive technique is used in 'A Man Asleep' (1967), the story of a disenchanted student who withdraws from social life. Only here Perec intensifies the level of detail by writing in the second person, *you*, building up slow and meticulous descriptions of the character's bedroom and the public spaces of his aimless walks.

Whether it is through short exercises of remembering or the epic survey of Paris that comprises *Lieux*, Perec's anthropological and autobiographical texts are structured and described through space. At the same time, those spaces – real or imaginary – are not stable worlds from which the writer can create stories. While space for Perec is the armature of experience, it remains fragile and ephemeral. As a result, meticulous attention to the physical realm is necessary in order to create character and to preserve it from erasure and disappearance. If Perec is so concerned that his characters are constructed by spaces and things, it is because the characters in themselves are incapable of remembrance. Space is the locus of memory (and history), and it must therefore be protected in order to prevent erasure. It must be described so that it may survive.

That survival is perhaps epitomised in *Species of Spaces*, 'a journal by a user of space', written in the style of Lewis Carroll, commissioned by Paul Virilio in 1973 and published the following year. This was the same year that Perec's friend and sometime collaborator Italo Calvino released *Invisible Cities*, another work that would ultimately offer a beautiful and oblique alternative to the assured and ordered worlds presented in so many architectural theories. *Species of Spaces* is a curious book, questioning, funny and disturbing. Across a series of short essays, Perec reflects on spatial issues, focusing on the analysis of everyday spaces – or, to use his term (and title of another piece), the 'infra-ordinary', as in the opposite of the extraordinary. He employs a rigorous structure of ascending scales, devoting each chapter to a separate species of space, one fitting inside the next like a Russian doll – from the space of the page to the bed, the bedroom, the flat, the building, the neighbourhood, the city, the countryside, the country, Europe, the Old Continent, the New Continent, the world and, finally, space.

The book opens with an image: the bellman's 'Ocean Chart' from Lewis Carroll's nonsensical poem 'The Hunting of the Snark', published in 1876. To begin with, it appears as a map of nothing – a blank sheet of paper – but the black perimeter of a rectangle transforms the emptiness into something new, with an inside and an outside. Perec's own writing has a similar way of cutting through space and becomes the vehicle for experiencing its limits:

> This is how space begins, with words only, signs traced on the blank page. To describe it: to name it, to trace it, like those portolano-makers who saturated the coastlines with the names of harbours, the names of capes, the names of inlets, until in the end the land was only separated from the sea by a continuous ribbon of text. Is the aleph, that place in Borges from which the entire world is visible simultaneously, anything other than an alphabet?[5]

Attention is required to step away from the usual point of view in order to see objectively. Perec asks naive questions about the way we divide and use our spaces: what is the meaning of the dotted line on a map that describes France, or 'when, in a given bedroom, you change the position of the bed, can you say you are changing rooms?' He laments the way in which we take space for granted, always assuming we know where we are (at home, at work, in the Metro, in the street). And yet we are not so bold with time: 'we are forever meeting people who have watches, very seldom people who have compasses' – a distinction that has well and truly collapsed with the smartphone, and arguably makes us even less attentive. If at first these observations seem childishly obvious, offering no generalisations or conclusions, that very naivety is his way of confronting the insensitivity with which we usually view the world. This is the only way he can expel preconceived ideas:

> It matters little to me that these questions should be fragmentary, barely indicative of a method, at most a project. It matters a lot to me that they should seem trivial and futile: that's exactly what makes them just as essential, if not more so, as all the other questions by which we've tried in vain to lay hold on our truth.[6]

Beyond its form as a catalogue or taxonomy of space, through the very study of these spaces, Perec is developing alternative ways of registering their existence. One technique, called 'Travaux pratiques', attempts to merge the observation and description of a place in Paris in a single act. As Perec describes what he sees while seated in a café, it is evident that the obstacles to seeing distinctly (a collective and personal deficiency) still anguish him: 'What we call quotidian is not clear, but opacity: a form of blindness, a form of anaesthesia.'[7] He proposes a method to extinguish this insensitivity: all preconceived ideas must be expelled; nothing should be taken for granted. Perec interrogates his space, establishing elementary distinctions: 'You must set about it more slowly, almost stupidly. Force yourself to write down what is of no interest, what is most obvious, most common, most colourless.'[8] While this attitude evokes the behaviour of the disengaged protagonist of 'A Man Asleep', the new project attempts to engage the viewer/protagonist with the space under observation, amassing and writing detail which, in aggregate, will embody that quotidian space. The most important aspect of the project is the simultaneity of perception and representation – methods Perec was exploring while working on *Lieux*.[9]

Along his journey from the micro to macro, Perec announces a series of projects, exercises in perception and description, that for the first time introduce enumeration, or the list, as an alternative to realist description. The first project, 'Lieux où j'ai dormi', proposes to describe all the places where he has slept. Perec claimed to remember them all, except those of his infancy. Although the texts are presented as accounts of real, observed phenomena, autobiography is their primary motive and, being based on remembered observation, they are twice translated, by perception and by memory, before they arrive as text on the page.

The wandering meditations of *Species of Spaces* inevitably return to childhood places, which offer themselves particularly well to 'the ineffable joys of enumeration' – putting elements into series or making micro-puzzles of things or events. An inventory, at least at the initial stage, means one is not *writing*. In silencing literature, the list brings into being a pure poetic structure that cannot be designed. Inventory becomes list, a list of litany or celebration. The remembered list offers not only the happiness of knowing, but also the knowledge of having ordered one's knowledge.

Perec's first experiment with enumeration was of the services found in an airport: 'there are deep armchairs and bench seats that aren't too comfortable...toilets...watchmakers and opticians'. The second list develops in a different, non-nominative manner, recording the present participles of verbs associated with moving house: 'fitting signing waiting imagining inventing investing deciding bending folding stooping...settling in living in'.[10] These experiments reveal one of the most significant characteristics of Perec's writing and one which continues through his subsequent work: the endowment of poetic purpose to words over and above their ability to describe the 'real' world from which they are taken. Enumeration enabled the rediscovery of one of the most original and effective poetic forms; to number, to order, to list is to catch the upheaval of thought. Michel Foucault argued that the Powers (Church, State, etc.) have used systems of classification to exclude and segregate. Perec, on the other hand, recrosses the same preoccupation at an empirical level, joining Sei Shōnagon's *Pillow Book*, the works of Rabelais and Lewis Carroll, or Jorge Luis Borges's encyclopaedic *Book of Imaginary Beings* in a similarly ludic and irrational means of representation, bringing together the real and the imaginary in a single space – a little like the pinned location on Google Maps of an imaginary place. The list effaces grammar, the sentence, the paragraph. It takes the word to the work in a single step, avoiding the need for a story or hierarchy. Temporality is removed from the text. Released from the requirement that it imitate the physical world, the emphasis of the list moves away from the object to the perceiver, creating a radical associative world that escapes the limits of description.

Lists and catalogues are also widely used in Perec's 1978 novel (or novels, as he called it) *Life A User's Manual*, which describes a Parisian building, removing the facade to leave every room and every resident (past and present) simultaneously visible, a single section from the ground floor to the garret. The building is ten storeys high and ten rooms wide, suggesting an expanded chessboard. Each room corresponds to a chapter. The order in which the chapters are sequenced is determined by the knight's tour, a system for moving the knight around a chessboard so that it alights on every square once and not more than once. For Perec this regulates a non-linear yet not entirely arbitrary spatial progression through the building. He then goes on to regulate the elements to be described in each room: inventories of objects, characters, actions, and allusions to other texts.

Literature is no safer from Perec's collector's instinct than anything else and informs much of the source material for each chapter. Many of his previous works and those of thirty selected writers are looted for details that reappear occasionally in the profusion of descriptions.

The book's six hundred pages and ninety-nine chapters develop around a specific moment: 23 June 1975, at approximately eight o'clock in the evening, on the third floor, when the central character, a wealthy Englishman named Bartlebooth, dies. Death takes Bartlebooth, fixing him and the entire apartment block in the moment of his own failure: he is incapable of completing the 439th puzzle of five hundred, a task to which he has dedicated his entire fortune and life.

The epic scale of Bartlebooth's project undeniably resembles Perec's *Lieux*: at age twenty he commits a decade to learning to paint with watercolours before spending twenty more years travelling the world, producing a watercolour of a different port every two weeks, totalling five hundred paintings. Each painting is then sent to France, where it is cut into a jigsaw puzzle by Gaspard Winckler who lives in a small flat in the upper levels of 11 Rue Simon-Crubellier. On returning from his travels, Bartlebooth dedicates his life to solving each puzzle and thus recreating the ports from his time abroad. Every completed puzzle is fixed with a special solution and sent to the port where it was first painted. Then the watercolour, twenty years after it was first painted, is soaked in a solution until its colours dissolve, leaving only a blank page and the outlines of the jigsaw before making its way back to Bartlebooth.

Beyond its scale, Bartlebooth's project also recalls *Lieux* in the mechanisms that define its realisation. The first of these is moral: the plan would not be an exploit or record, neither a peak to scale nor an ocean floor to trawl. Bartlebooth's project would not be heroic or spectacular, but rather simple and discreet. The plan would be difficult, of course, but not impossibly so, controlled from the start to the finish and conversely controlling every detail of the life of the man engaged upon it. The second is logical: all recourse to chance would be ruled out. Both projects would make time and space serve as the abstract coordinates plotting the repetition of identical events occurring in their allotted spaces, on their allotted dates. The third is aesthetic: the plan would be useless, since gratuitousness was the sole guarantor of its rigour, and would destroy itself as it proceeded; its perfection would be circular: a series of events which when completed nullify each other. Starting from nothing, passing through precise operations on finished objects, Bartlebooth would end up with nothing.[11]

But the principal similarity between *Lieux* and Bartlebooth's endeavour is the way in which both seek to programme time over a prolonged period in relation to displacement in space. The function of such programming seems to be one of protecting the author from the future by consuming it in advance. Within this, the two projects share the desire to accumulate, whether through objects, texts or watercolours.

If in terms of their chronology and their method of execution the proximity of *Lieux* and Bartlebooth's watercolours/puzzles suggests a certain kinship, their respective ambitions could not be further apart. For *Lieux*, Perec undertook a one-way journey culminating in the collation of texts for publication. Even if the purpose of the project was to observe a process of ageing, the writing took place in real time, working against forgetfulness, stopping the past from disappearing and constructing a framework for future memory.

Lieux had aspirations similar to those of the diary; a hope incompatible with the solipsism of Bartlebooth's project, which, despite involving a very long journey around the world, never looks outside itself for evidence of being. The project can only conclude by his death or by the erasure of all that was produced during his life (the destruction of his watercolours). Bartlebooth's project involves competition with another, Gaspard Winckler the puzzle maker, who eventually triumphs (albeit a posthumous victory), which might explain why he, and not Bartlebooth, is named on Google Maps. Finally, half of the texts in *Lieux* were to be generated from memory, whereas Bartlebooth produces watercolours directly from five hundred ports around the world before coming home to reconstruct his memories of nothing. Bartlebooth, being a character of fiction, whose project and history can go to the end of desperation, shows the absurdity of life itself. He finishes his outgoing journey, succeeding where another neighbour, Serge Valène, fails. Valène, who wants to make a giant painting of the building in section with all its residents, dies in front of an almost blank canvas.

While lists proliferate through *Life A User's Manual*, the novel also depends on description to set each character in the world: the description of ten objects in each room (or chapter) is, for example, one of the many constraints that enables the writing of the book. In this case, all of the objects are invented, removing any necessity to translate real phenomena into textual form, even though much of the description could pass for realist. But *Life A User's Manual* differs from *Lieux* in its dependence on literary conventions, making the link to a referential world a secondary consideration. Unsurprisingly, the book's structure lends itself particularly well to the use of lists. Its formal organization demands that forty-two elements (objects, characters, actions, references) be described in each chapter; the list provides the author with a systematic way of uniting these heterogeneous elements. Lists of the objects stored in the residents' basements perfectly mirror the novel's own apparently haphazard accumulations, while simultaneously revealing the characters who are hidden from view by their self-consciously arranged apartments:

> The Altamonts' cellar, clean, tidy, and neat: from floor to ceiling, shelving and pigeon-holes labelled in large, legible letters. A place for every thing, and every thing in its place; nothing has been left out: wheat flour, semolina, cornflower...tinned fish, tuna chunks... the so-called table wines, then the Beaujolais ...detergents, descaling liquid...
>
> The Gratiolets' cellar. Here generations have heaped up rubbish unsorted and

unordered by anyone...the base and posts of an empire bed, hickorywood skis having lost their spring long ago, a pith helmet that was the purest white once upon a time.[12]

Despite the close attention to the everyday that anchors Perec's writing in the real world, his lists bring together dreaming and thinking. Their effect depends as much on what is omitted as what is included; he knows that classification can be the enemy of liberty and what goes unfinished emancipates. More interesting are the dispersed facts he collects, only exceptionally reaching back to familiar knowledge, placing them in the category reserved for the miscellaneous. They constitute urgent zones, about which we know only that we know little and where one senses that a great deal could be found if one decided to lend them some attention: banal facts, passed under an unclaimed silence. They describe us, even if we think we can dispense from writing them down.[13] Like Borges's *Book of Imaginary Beings*, Perec's lists destroy accepted knowledge and question the categories which 'tame the wild profusion of existing things'.[14] Enumeration distinguishes between the real and the imaginary, while allowing them to share the same space. The system of ordering things enables the imagination to accommodate ludicrous juxtapositions. The 'mere act of enumeration that heaps them all together has a power of enchantment of its own'.[15] Words such as 'in', 'and' or 'on' suggest that things can exist together in the world, but enumeration removes the reassurance that things can be located within language or in the space of the page. Enumeration removes the need for the world to provide an acceptable container within which things can be brought together. The list acknowledges the autonomy of language in relation to the physical world.

The Perecian journey through space has slowly transformed itself into a journey from the writer's city, Paris, to language, where memory and place are always present and constantly overlapping. In projects such as *Lieux*, Perec was developing a phenomenological method that would accurately reflect observed reality in language. Despite his commitment to the everyday life, he gradually moved his allegiance away from phenomena, towards language and words. The stories told in *Life A User's Manual* are suggested by thinking and remembering the space in which the events took place. The rooms of the building allow Perec to suspend and compress time, to situate each character in their own space before they are sent off beyond the building into the spaces of the past. The book operates like a map. A story's spatial coordinates must be given before its telling. The book unfolds over a brief moment, when every character is situated, stationary, within various parts of the building, with the exception of Valène who slowly climbs the stairs. Each chapter is named after the occupant of the space it represents, except for the chapters on the few collective spaces (staircases, lifts and lobbies) named according to their functions. Each chapter starts with a meticulous description of its room, making it visible and purposeful. Every possible detail is given, gradually building up an image of the current occupant. As a detail is developed – a story or memory is evoked by the person who took the photograph on the wall, or the name of a manufacturer engraved on a piece of furniture – the text changes direction, becoming an exploration of past events. Description quickly moves away from the present inhabitant to a previous one, or a person who is altogether foreign to the building but who has nevertheless managed to leave a mark. The current resident becomes subjectified within the historical space of the room as the story transgresses its physical boundaries. The author navigates the space of the chess board, dematerialising its grid as each tale is recounted.

Bartlebooth designs his project to give his life a purpose. It was meant to be challenging yet achieve nothing, occupy his entire life and take him to more places around the world than any other character in the book (with the exception of Smautf, Bartlebooth's faithful butler, who accompanies him). His displacements prevent him from leaving any traces or making memories. Despite his five hundred puzzles of places visited, Bartlebooth has no relationship with them – the spaces have not defined him and they in turn have not provided him with a site for his memories, only mysteries. Above all, his project reflects the futility of his life.

As for Valène, he numbers and records every story told in preparation for his painting. During the instant in which the book is set, the moment of Bartlebooth's death, Valène is climbing the stairs of the building, remembering and reconstructing each stor(e)y, floor by floor, resident by resident. He has lived here longer than anyone. Ascending the flights, he is the trustee of collective recollections.

> Yes, it could begin this way, right here, just like that, in a rather slow and ponderous way, in this neutral place that belongs to all and to none, where people pass by almost without seeing each other, where the life of the building regularly and distantly resounds.[16]

> On the stairs the furtive shadows pass of all those who were once there....
> He tried to resuscitate those imperceptible details which over the course of fifty-five years had woven the life of this house and which the years had unpicked one by one.... The stairs, for him, were on each floor, a memory, an emotion, something ancient and impalpable, something palpitating somewhere in the guttering flame of his memory.[17]

When Valène reaches the third floor, Bartlebooth's, he remembers the dying old man in one of the book's most striking scenes. He muses on the passage of time, the passage of people repeatedly moving in and out of the building. The stairs become the silent witness to the removal companies, the undertakers, every visit for minor maintenance or major renovation work, the presence of one occupant effacing the previous one. The building is a memorial to all those people he has recounted and it is a memorial to himself. It provides the armature for the compilation of lives which will make his painting. The spaces are evidence of the freezing of time and of the (re)construction of the lives within them.

> Sometimes Valène had the feeling that time had stopped, suspended, frozen around he didn't know what expectation. The very idea of the picture he planned to do and whose laid-out, broken-up images had begun to haunt every second of his life, furnishing his dreams, squeezing his memories, the very idea of this shattered building laying bare the cracks of its past, the crumbling of its present, this unordered amassing of stories grandiose and trivial, frivolous and pathetic, gave him the impression of a grotesque mausoleum raised in memory of companions petrified in terminal postures as insignificant in their solemnity as they were in their ordinariness, as he had wanted both to warn of and delay these slow or quick deaths which seemed to be engulfing the entire building storey by storey.[18]

Unusually, the enlargement of the space outside the building continues as an excavation of the future. Valène's dreams about death invade him as he projects them forward, casting doubt on the building's ability to retain something permanent. He resigns himself, in the end, to the inevitable disappearance of the building and the insensitivity with which the city and its speculators will cover its traces:

> The street will be no more than a string of blind facades – bleak walls, vacant eye-like windows – alternating with poster-patched palisades and nostalgic graffiti.... The tireless bulldozers of the site-levellers will come to shovel off the rest: tonnes and tonnes of scree and dust.[19]

The passage recalls the distress expressed by Perec in both *Species of Spaces* and *Lieux*. The disappearance of Rue Vilin, recorded in *Lieux*, cruelly erased forever the presence of his family and his childhood in the city. Only when rewriting his memories could they be situated in a more stable space. While Valène is the only conscious occupant of the collective spaces in *Life A User's Manual*, his space is described in terms of the lives and memories of others; his dreams are buried under theirs. All the spaces of the building are fused in his consciousness. The artist slowly makes his way up the building, interrupted by journeys to places around the world, spanning hundreds of years – a journey in its own right that points to the decentred and fragmented worlds examined in *Species of Spaces* and *Lieux*. Valène speaks the unspeakable, representing a collective voice. Through him, Perec articulates the notion of space as an armature for the self to experience and remember the world.

He invents a character who is only visible when situated by others who are in turn situated by their spaces, present and past. Perec disguises space in journeys through time, constantly trying to stabilise it so that it may be lived in and remembered.

Postscript
Lieux was a way for Perec to record the passage of time. Not to describe the passage of time but for time to be the structure of the work. It would simultaneously record the ageing of places, and in some cases their disappearance, the ageing of his memories, as they became more distant with each rewriting, and the ageing of his writing. When I wrote the first version of this essay in 1996, it was also neatly topical; *Species of Spaces* had not yet been translated.[20] I felt I had discovered something genuinely new to write about, in the English-speaking world at least. This piece as it now appears contains most of what was later published in AA *Files* and the review of *Species of Spaces* that I wrote for the *Architects' Journal* in 1997. Today there is so much more scholarship around Perec that the essay feels rather naive. Then again, for all its shortcomings, I recognise some of the enthusiasm I had for the subject, the thrill of reading wild experiments by Perec and friends in the OuLiPo. But for all the mind-boggling complexity and playfulness of Perec's constraints, his writing remains melancholic, reflecting the sadness of his short life.

In matters of style, the piece can still feel a bit clunky. I remember working with AA *Files* editor Mark Rappolt, who was tough and asked for several rewrites. Close to publication, a third of the text had to be cut due to overlaps with the far superior essay by Paul Auster on the same subject,[21] which arrived late. Even in this newly revised essay I can see how different elements of the much longer text have been grafted together and leave their own scars. But in the end, including it here is an accidental micro case study on the very subject which Perec was examining in *Lieux* – the passing of time and its effect on space, memory and writing.

In 2022, *Lieux* was finally published in full by Seuil. The book is a beautiful 'monster', as Perec had predicted in a letter to Maurice Nadeau in 1969. An accompanying website collects all the completed texts, which can be searched by place and date, real or imagined, and reassembled in any way the reader may choose. Perec would have loved the internet, for *Lieux* at least. In acting against forgetfulness, his spatial and temporal intuitions were remarkably prescient.

1. Georges Perec, 'Species of Spaces', in *Species of Spaces and Other Pieces*, trans. John Sturrock (London: Penguin, 1997), 91.
2. For a fuller description of *Life A User's Manual*, see Paul Auster, 'The Bartlebooth Follies', AA *Files* 45/46 (2001): 88–89.
3. Philippe Lejeune, *La Mémoire et l'oblique: Georges Perec autobiographe* (Paris: POL, 1991).
4. For the development of this theme in the work of Perec prior to *Lieux*, see Enrique Walker's interview 'Virilio on Perec', AA *Files* 45/46 (2001): 15–18.
5. Perec, 'Species of Spaces', 13.
6. Ibid., 211.
7. Georges Perec, *Espèces d'espaces* (Paris: Editions Galilée, 1974), inside front cover.
8. Perec, 'Species of Spaces', 50.
9. For a fuller description of *Lieux*, see Andrew Leak, 'Paris: Created and Destroyed', AA *Files* 45/46 (2001): 25–31.
10. Perec, 'Species of Spaces', 36.
11. Georges Perec, *Life A User's Manual*, trans. David Bellos (London: Collins Harvill, 1987), 118.
12. Perec, *Life A User's Manual*, 153, 155.
13. Georges Perec, *Penser/classer* (Paris: Hachette, 1985), 156.
14. Michel Foucault, *The Order of Things: An Archaeology of the Human Sciences* (New York: Vintage, 1994), xv.
15. Ibid., 5.
16. Perec, *Life A User's Manual*, 3.
17. Ibid., 59–62.
18. Ibid., 127.
19. Ibid., 130–31.
20. *Species of Spaces* was published in English in 1997 by Penguin Classics. It is a great translation by John Thurrock and contains many other texts not included in the French edition of 1974. I reviewed it for the *Architects' Journal* in February 1998, my first published piece.
21. Paul Auster wrote the 'The Bartlebooth Follies' in the same issue, which was reprinted after first appearing in the *New York Times* in 1987.

Combines two articles: 'From Lieux to Life...', published in AA *Files* 45/46, 2001, double issue dedicated to Georges Perec, reprinted in AA *Files* X, 2018; 'New Perspectives on Familiar Spaces', review of *Species of Spaces and Other Pieces* by Georges Perec, translated by John Sturrock, in *Architects' Journal*, February 1998

Dirty Old River
A Short Walk Along the Thames

London is very good at many things, but public space is not one of them. London, essentially, is a trading city with little time or energy for civic representation compared with other European capitals. However, if we look for private spaces that are publicly accessible, we are in with a chance, and I would head straight for the royal parks and gardens, easily among the best in the western world. Another exception is the top deck (preferably the front seat) of a double decker bus going from anywhere to anywhere. But perhaps the best way of encountering London is on a walk along the Thames, ideally a loop along both banks. While we may pass noteworthy public art and architecture, the real artwork is the city itself, eccentrically built in a series of competitive collisions and accidents that reveal its nature, politics and its people.

Waterloo Bridge

London's unruly temperament has never accepted grand urban gestures or masterplans. Even Christopher Wren failed. The ink had barely dried on his design for a baroque plan for the City of London following the Great Fire of 1666 when merchants rebuilt their properties on the medieval footprint. Not even the financial power of City banks can regularise a plot for skyscrapers. The most they can expect from Londoners is to be affectionately nicknamed Gherkin, Walkie-Talkie or Cheese Grater. Across the river, skateboarders stopped a campaign to turn all culture into retail. Even when stretches of riverbank are dull – and they frequently are – the space made by the Thames is worth it. More than the parks, the river creates a void in the city, a space full of nature and history but empty of humans, which is so rare anywhere else. The muddy water makes it uncanny; precisely framed yet naturally formed. And to walk in a loop creates a cinematic experience; the space you pass through becomes a panoramic picture from the opposite bank a few minutes later.

You can easily make your own route by choosing which bridges define the loop. The longest loop, from Tower Bridge to Vauxhall Bridge, is about fifteen kilometres, then the loops shorten by around one to two kilometres with each bridge omitted. Here I will take you from Blackfriars Bridge to Vauxhall Bridge (approximately eight-and-a-half kilometres), starting in Lincoln's Inn Fields. The walk hugs the riverbank, and you are only ever a few steps away from the water except where the Houses of Parliament and MI6 annoyingly grab the riverfront for themselves. Along the way there are many tempting diversions inland. Some are elegantly signalled by grand tree-lined vistas while others are barely visible alleys and undercrofts. Follow your heart. London rewards the adventurer more than the scholar.

With adventure in mind, this walk is light on tour guide facts. For GPS-located, hard historical information on buildings and architects, use the fantastic and free London Architecture Guide app that puts the classic *Guide to the Architecture of London* by Ed Jones and Christopher Woodward into your phone. For a more analogue and emotional companion, *Nairn's London* is an extraordinary love letter to the city. So many places and buildings have changed or disappeared since it was published in 1966, but to read and feel the loss amplifies Ian Nairn's genuine affection for and occasional rage at his subject. And perhaps more for a read in the park before or after a walk, *London's Natural History*, written just after the Second World War by RSR Fitter, is still unrivalled in showing that, despite the best efforts of Londoners to prove otherwise, nature is still boss.

Lincoln's Inn Fields to Victoria Embankment

Start in wonderful Lincoln's Inn Fields, London's oldest square and one of its greatest, full of interesting and quirky specimen trees dotted among huge London planes, the city's arboreal cockney of choice. For the ultimate architectural primer to a London walk, visit Sir John Soane's Museum on the north side of the square.

Away from the banks of the Thames, London is always rising and falling around the myriad of small rivers that define many of the neighbourhoods long after they have been covered from view. From the southeast corner of the Lincoln's Inn Fields, zigzag downhill to the river through the smallest lanes you can find. If it is open, walk through the Inns of Court for a brief architectural history of London in squares, gardens, halls and elegant terraces. When the teaching of law was banned from the City of London in the thirteenth century, the lawyers moved just outside the City limits to the hamlet of Holborn where they work to this day. Keep heading downhill and you will reach the Thames on Victoria Embankment. A pair of cast iron dragons marks the boundary of the City.

Sir John Soane's Museum, 1792–1823

Victoria Embankment

Cross the busy road to reach the riverside. Look carefully at the water; is it flowing in or out? High or low? The Thames rises and falls by up to seven metres per tide. I like it best at the lowest tide, when the riverbed is visible and reveals lots of great fragments of maritime infrastructure. Check on it regularly as you go. This is the natural foundation of London. This section of the Embankment is somewhat unremarkable, but it is a great place to get your bearings thanks to the bend in the river. Although the Thames runs roughly east–west through the city, its serpentine trajectory means it is very rarely running east–west at any single point, making orientation by riverbank unreliable.

Here, like the top or bottom of every bend, you will catch many different views of London at once. To the east is the City, marked by the aggressively inelegant 20 Fenchurch Street, better known as the Walkie-Talkie for its handset-like form (Rafael Viñoly, 2014). The much finer Shard (Renzo Piano, 2012) by London Bridge marks the moment when high-value capital jumped from the North to the South Bank, no doubt encouraged by Tate Modern (Herzog & de Meuron, 2000 and 2016), which occupies Giles Gilbert Scott's Bankside Power Station (1947–63), its chimney also in view. An assortment of inoffensive towers rises behind the South Bank directly on the other side. Looking west, you will see the London Eye and Big Ben beyond Waterloo Bridge.

Take a right, heading west. Stop before you reach Somerset House. If you are walking at twilight or later, this is a nice place to watch the bright interiors of double decker buses cross Waterloo Bridge like inhabited lanterns.

Cross the road to walk close to the amazing Palladian base of Somerset House (William Chambers, 1776). Before the Embankment was built (1865–70), the huge pillars and arches stood in the river itself, allowing one to arrive into the building by boat, tide permitting.

You are now walking on one of London's most important pieces of engineered infrastructure. The Victoria Embankment, designed by Joseph Bazalgette, combines roads and gardens aboveground, a sewer and an underground railway. All of this is mostly out of view, except for the street furniture, particularly the fabulous dolphins that twist around the cast iron lamps designed by George John Vulliamy (1870), which line this whole walk more or less in step with the London plane trees. In spring and summer their canopies touch, creating a continuous ceiling. Watch out for camels and sphinxes on benches and the rather surreal tourist magnet of Cleopatra's Needle (c. 1450 BCE), which apparently has its twin in Central Park.

Mulberry tree, Victoria Embankment Gardens, 1874, built on reclaimed land following Bazalgette's Embankment and sewer

You might want to cross the road a few times if traffic allows. The elongated gardens built on the Embankment are pretty in a super-Victorian way, especially Victoria Embankment Gardens with its floral railings, annual flower beds and fantastic ancient trees. There's a grand old mulberry tree whose long branches are as thick as the trunk, so old and heavy that they have to be propped up with metal crutches like a Zimmer frame. Old tyres are perfectly formed to help cushion. I wonder if it could be one of the park's original residents? There are also Indian bean trees, cherry trees, palm trees and many other exotic and native plants you might expect on a proper Victorian constitutional. Of all the important men on plinths – in the Victorian garden, a phenomenon that is as natural as trees – look out for the smallest and most modest: a bust relief by Mary Grant of the economist and reformer Henry Fawcett, husband of Millicent Garrett Fawcett, the leader of England's women's suffrage movement for half a century. His closed blind eyes are movingly unheroic. It was installed in 1888, just a few years after the Embankment was built, and it would take another 130 years before Millicent would make it onto Parliament Square.

You will pass under or over seven bridges along this walk. Each one is interesting in its own right. Look up at the structure overhead and the piers rising from the water holding it in place. The weight of the bridge seems like nothing compared with the never-ending forces of the tides. At Hungerford Bridge cracks in brickwork and the oversized cornice evoke an ancient ruin. Until the eighteenth century, there were only two bridges across the Thames: London Bridge and another much further west, at Kingston. Many were proposed but were blocked by the powerful Guild of Watermen who controlled the huge economy of river crossings.

Westminster

Approaching Westminster, you feel the power of government before you can actually see it. Architecturally the Ministry of Defence (E. Vincent Harris, 1951, same year as the Royal Festival Hall) makes the first monumental move with its strange cocktail of Modern-Georgian. Quite successful in a fuck-you kind of way. Chandos House meets Fascist Como for the archi-geeks.

Next is New Scotland Yard – don't miss the classic rotating triangular sign designed by Edward Wright in 1968 and relocated from Victoria when the Metropolitan Police moved headquarters in 2016.

Portcullis House (Hopkins, 2001) is where we start to pick up the first postmodern signs of the walk, which will peak at Vauxhall. Michael and Patty Hopkins, who would never describe themselves as postmodernists, turned away from their super-refined high-tech of the 1970s and 80s to a more establishment-friendly, heavy Victorian-engineering-inspired monumentality that made an uneasy entry into British architecture at the turn of the millennium but now seems to be mellowing well. Westminster underground station (also by Hopkins) is a must if you haven't travelled through it. It is a dizzying three-dimensional journey into the new underworld of the Jubilee Line. Piranesi meets Gotham City. I'm surprised we haven't seen it in more films.

A tutor at architecture school once described the Palace of Westminster (Charles Barry and Augustus Pugin, 1860) as the most pompous building in London. I'm not sure I agree but my view of it has been tainted ever since. And yet looking at it on this walk has lanced my prejudice. As you make your way around it, be sure to extract the Gothic Westminster Hall (1401) from the visual fizz of neo-Gothic stonework. Consult any guide to London for more info. It is fun also to imagine the kind of culture that might have emerged had John Soane's neoclassical design been built instead (which you can see in his house-museum on Lincoln's Inn Fields).

Across the road, the Abbey and Westminster School. On Parliament Square, British political history is represented by eleven men and one woman: the statue of Millicent Garrett Fawcett by Gillian Wearing was erected in 2018. Eyes wide open, banner in hand, she stares straight at Parliament. The whole space is corralled by the now ubiquitous urban vernacular of black steel anti-terrorist obstructions, worthy of an architectural study of their own.

Things calm down once you pass Victoria Tower at the southern end of the Palace of Westminster and enter Victoria Tower Gardens. Given the location, it is a refreshingly informal space. A statue of Emmeline Pankhurst (1930, moved here in 1958) greets you as you enter.

Millicent Garrett Fawcett, by Gillian Wearing, Parliament Square, 2018

Dirty Old River

Here she stands more serene-looking than the activist who was photographed struggling against the arms of a policeman outside Buckingham Palace in 1914. Note also the relief of her daughter Christabel Pankhurst, added to the plinth when the sculpture was moved from a different location in the gardens in 1958 (Christabel's more radical socialist sister Sylvia is modestly commemorated in Mile End Park, Bethnal Green). Nearby, an original casting of Rodin's *Burghers of Calais* (1908–15) renders pain and sacrifice collective. Six figures with nooses around their necks await their fate to save their city. The sculpture commemorates the end of the siege of Calais by the English during the Hundred Years' War in the fourteenth century. King Edward III demanded that six prominent burghers of the town offer their lives to spare the people of the city. While making the sculptures, Rodin erected several scaffolding plinths in the garden of his studio to determine the ideal height from which to encounter the six burghers as they faced imminent death – starting from the ground itself and up to around four metres high. He had wanted the work to be low, but both the times and patrons demanded something with more authority. Here in Victoria Tower Gardens, the low plinth gives the whole space an intimacy made even more affecting by the distant sound of children playing in the swings and sandpits at the southern end. And it puts the men on Parliament Square in perspective – literally. How different things might be if history wasn't always looking down at us.

Burghers of Calais, by Auguste Rodin, 1908–15

Before leaving the park, return to the river's edge and look across from under the trees; St Thomas's Hospital and the Lambeth Palace are much more visible from here than when you walk past them in a few minutes. The three handsome Italianate pavilion ward blocks (Henry Currey, 1871) are what remain of the hospital, one of the first to be designed following Florence Nightingale's 'pavilion principle', which separated beds and improved ventilation.

Tate Britain

After leaving the park, continue along the river. Past Lambeth Bridge is Millbank Tower (Ronald Ward, 1963), a classic 1960s glass and steel corporate complex rising from a horizontal base. Not worth stopping but worth remembering fondly given the horrors you will witness in a moment upriver. But before all that, Tate Britain, whose Clore Gallery extension (Stirling and Wilford, 1987) is one the very best postmodern buildings in Britain. A bright blue duct poking out provoca-

Rear of the Clore Gallery, Tate Britain, Stirling and Wilford, 1987

tively from the unassuming back announces the collage of architectural elements brought together to form the gallery extension. Outtakes of the two neighbouring buildings collide in the entrance and flank; Tate's neoclassical pediment is inverted to form a void of the same shape for the entrance but, at street level this time, avoids monumentality like Rodin. The Edwardian red brick and stone quoins building on the riverside produces a tartan of matching materials. Inside, the space and details are freer, an exuberant architectural promenade with bold colours leading you from place to place until you reach the more restrained galleries where the Turners hang.

Vauxhall

From Tate Britain, walk over Vauxhall Bridge and stop in the middle. Heaven and Hell right here. Check the water. Higher or lower? Still flowing. Heaven first: the view looking north, wide and open. A big sky over the whole city. And to your right, the wackiest large government building there is: MI6 (Terry Farrell, 1993) seems to use the same technique of dazzle patterns found on war ships. The deep green glass and stone ziggurat is so bizarre that one fails to notice it is the HQ of British counterintelligence. Talk about hiding in plain sight. But any postmodern excess one may enjoy is destroyed by the real estate crimes lining the river's South Bank and the Nine Elms development at your back.

Turn around and you will see how capital can ruin a city. The new American Embassy (Kieran Timberlake, 2017) sets the bombastic tone with an absurd cube of architectural gimmickry barricaded within its own citadel. (Remember the elegant civic modernism of its former Eero Saarinen-designed home on Grosvenor Square, now being converted into a luxury hotel). Developers have heaped on more and more sellable area at the expense of any civic quality, with buildings standing like profit bars on a financial spreadsheet.

Nine Elms hell, 2021

Lambeth

Walking from Vauxhall to Lambeth is uneventful. The Inca-inspired stone piers surrounding MI6 remain perplexing and lead to a pleasant stretch long enough for the anger to subside as long as you look towards the river. Once back on the Embankment, the dolphin lamps are with you again. Street names give some sense of how different the story of London is south of the river: Glasshouse Walk, Tinworth Street and other trades are a world away from the dukes and earls naming Westminster.

If you are looking for more art and can't wait until the Southbank Centre, take a detour into Newport Street where you will find Damien Hirst's gallery and restaurant. Designed by Caruso St John (2016), it is one of the best architectural projects in London this century. Subtle

RIP Cherry Tree, 2021

and strong, it fuses together a series of former industrial buildings, creating a wonderfully irregular sequence of gallery spaces. This is an exemplary model of reuse.

Across the road from Lambeth Bridge, the Garden Museum, converted and extended by Dow Jones (2008 and 2017) with gardens by Dan Pearson, is well worth a visit. Beyond it, Lambeth Palace places the Archbishop of Canterbury within striking distance of Parliament.

Continue along the river. Just before the imposing wall which surrounds St Thomas's Hospital, stop to look across at where you have just come from. For many years a great cherry tree marked the spot; more recently, a new sapling has been planted in its place. It may be cheesy, but this is one of the most iconic views of London. The Palace of Westminster, reflected in the river at high tide, with the triple standard lamps marching across Westminster Bridge. The narrow walk along St Thomas's Hospital oversailed by the continuous canopy of large London plane trees is wonderfully peaceful. Remember Florence.

Passing under Westminster Bridge you reach County Hall (1922 and 1933). No need to stop as the building is so big you can easily experience its Edwardian-Baroque without breaking step. Now home to myriad amusements, it was built to house London regional government, first the London County Council (LCC), then Greater London Council (GLC), before it was abolished by Margaret Thatcher in 1985 in a bitter battle for power across the Thames. Until then, London's public realm was determined inside County Hall. With only a few exceptions, every architect worth their salt worked for the LCC. Many buildings of the postwar period which now credit their architects by name were in fact designed by the council.

Note that the dolphin lamps are still with us but dated 1911, then 1933.

London Eye

Millennial bauble. Go for a ride if the fancy takes you.

Southbank Centre to Blackfriars Bridge

Hungerford Bridge leads to the great set piece of welfare state architecture. But big-brand commerce has ruined the lightness of the Royal Festival Hall (LCC, GLC, the great and the good of British architecture and design, 1951), so let's move on to the Queen Elizabeth Hall, Purcell Room and Hayward Gallery (LCC, GLC, 1967). A collection of rough concrete forms with little discernible logic which provoked a rare scorn from the authors of the London Architecture Guide. 'The concert hall', they write, 'is an ugly room: more concrete, no decoration, and unsympathetic lighting', while 'the lobby common to both halls works badly, and shuffling queues always form at the entrances to the auditoria. This is particularly strange, as part of the rationale of "organic" architecture of this sort is that each space or form should be tailored specifically to suit its function.' While I cannot defend the buildings against functional criticism, I always find them thrilling. Each awkward building form is almost animalistic. You can find personalities and poses all around. The array of glass pyramid rooflights over the Hayward, best enjoyed from the top deck of a bus, could have easily inspired the haircut of choice for punks. And while the lack of entrance from the Embankment is confusing, it has produced a wonderfully strange undercroft used since the 1990s by skateboarders who successfully campaigned against the space being turned into more commerce.

Perched atop the Hayward is the more recent arrival of Dan Graham's glass pavilion *Waterloo Sunset*, named after The Kinks' 1967 London classic song – a nice prompt for those with headphones and Spotify to stop on one of the many raised decks and listen while looking over the Thames. 'Dirty old river, must you keep rolling...'

Still more to see: the hundreds of secondhand books laid out atop rows of foldable tables would be pulp without the cover of Waterloo Bridge. Just beyond, the red carpeted foyers and concrete cantilevers of the

National Theatre (Denys Lasdun, 1977) seem almost camp, like so much of the 1970s. The dolphin lamps along this stretch are dated 1964, but the plane trees seem younger. If you are lucky enough to walk at low tide, a wonderful beach is accessible. From the sandy, muddy shore, the city feels more geological than architectural.

Now, up the steep steps beside candy-coloured Blackfriars Bridge for a last look down the river before heading back down the Embankment. A pretty, pale blue police calling box and red telephone box stand on the banks of the Thames, as out of time as Cleopatra's Needle. Little details normally invisible in the constant excitement of people-watching jump out as remarkable. Railings, paving and blossom are one and the same with monuments and tidal forces. How tightly bound the making of London is with its nature. The river will be around two metres higher or lower than when you started thanks to lunar and other celestial pulls, unless you timed it around the turning of tides. It takes five to seven hours for a tide to rise or fall completely, launching or returning the thousands of ships that made the city – a city that has changed even when it behaves as it always has.

Blue police call box

Low tide, 2021

Dirty Old River

Partially published in 2021 by *Frieze* online, www.frieze.com/city-guides/london

ns, Grids and Ghosts
From Stowe to Milton Keynes

Stowe

A visitor to Stowe buys a ticket and picks up a map at the coaching inn built on the edge of the estate before beginning a tour of one of the great English gardens. The tour begins with an approach down a mile-long drive flanked on either side by woods. At the end of this grand avenue is an arch in the Corinthian order which frames a view of Stowe House and a great sweep of countryside beyond. This 'countryside' is of course all garden – shaped largely by Capability Brown's naturalistic gestures, with ponds posing as lakes and rivers, sheep held between invisible folds in the land, clumps of trees and arrangements of statues, and one of the defining prototypes of the English landscape tradition. Widely admired and endlessly copied in public parks and gardens across the world, Stowe and its contemporaries were the visible expression of the philosophical watershed of the Enlightenment, heralding the birth of aesthetics and an emphasis on individual experience that to a large extent still defines the condition in which we live today.

Although visitors come to Stowe to see the gardens, the house plays a crucial role as the primary point of view in structuring the landscape and the placement of its signature ha-ha. Between one and two metres deep, this asymmetrical ditch stretches across the entire width of the estate and is arguably the most radical invention of modern architecture. Its purpose was to keep animals and undesirables away from the house without disturbing the view. With a vertical retaining wall on the house side and a gentle grassy slope on the other, the ha-ha was fundamental to the illusion of boundlessness in the English garden. Consider it the eighteenth-century ancestor of the modernist obsession with vast, frameless windows blurring the division between inside and outside. While the infinite view offered by the ha-ha was reserved for the family and their guests, the visiting public entered from the 'wrong' side and were offered a practical and rhetorical choice: follow the path of virtue or the path of vice or the path of Liberty. Vice follows works of architecture and sculpture devoted to pleasure. The virtuous side of the garden, in contrast, is designed to edify and educate rather than amuse, and leads you face-to-face with the political and moral ideals of eighteenth-century British culture. Liberty celebrates military heroes.

What makes Stowe so different from other gardens is its political dimension. In this sense it was a form of slow-motion propaganda, a manifestation of power, but not of the absolute, monarchical French kind, exemplified by the divine axis at Versailles leading directly to the chambers of the Sun King, but something more

Palladian Bridge, Stowe

Gardens, Grids and Ghosts

explicitly British. At Stowe, the heart of this national identity are the Elysian Fields, laid out by William Kent in 1734, a densely symbolic landscape and home to a series of monuments, statues and follies, the most famous of which is the Temple of British Worthies, featuring busts of Alexander Pope, Thomas Gresham, Inigo Jones, John Milton, William Shakespeare, John Locke, Isaac Newton, Francis Bacon, Walter Raleigh, Francis Drake, John Hampden, John Barnard and a handful of monarchs.

As the fame of Stowe spread, it quickly established itself as a place people longed to visit, including US presidents John Adams and Thomas Jefferson, who would become the driving forces in the reconception of the modern American landscape. Of course, other than an American political class and members of the aristocracy, the only people who had time to make such pilgrimages were the growing ranks of the English upper-middle class, who enjoyed the pleasure of time at their disposal or what today we might call 'leisure'. The willingness of the resident Temple-Grenville family to open these private gardens to the public was unprecedented. By the end of the eighteenth century more than two thousand people were visiting the gardens each year, at the same moment Britain was making its first tentative steps towards an idea of leisure and public space, a concept and practice with which it has continued to maintain an uneasy relationship. The scale of the operation demanded the first-ever guidebook to a country estate. *A Description of the Gardens of Lord Viscount Cobham* by Benton Seeley (1744) was published as a profusely illustrated volume describing the details and history of the things that could be found there.

Milton Keynes

Out of sight, but only twenty miles to the east, is another cultivated landscape committed to the public good, in many ways equal to Stowe in terms of both political purpose and leisurely consequence. But where Stowe is a landscape constructed to simulate nature for political ends, Milton Keynes's political aims were in a landscape constructed to simulate the city. This apparent oxymoron is even embedded in its founding slogan, to make a city 'greener than the surrounding countryside', and in the appealing misconception that its name synthesises two more British worthies – John Milton and John Maynard Keynes (rather than the less romantic but nevertheless actual source of its name, the nearby village of Middleton de Caiynes) – and as such represents a great burst of late 1960s utopian thinking in which modern architecture and picturesque planning are intertwined in multiple and often contradictory ways.

Evoking something between indifference and derision everywhere except in the city itself – the fruits of modernism never having been easily assimilated by the empirical English – Milton Keynes remains a fitting place to reflect on the many lives of the English landscape. Arguably Milton Keynes represents the most radical experiment in architecture and landscape since the end of the Second World War, a testament to the enlightened welfare state just as Stowe was to the Enlightenment of the eighteenth century.

Arriving at Milton Keynes Central railway station, a visitor is greeted by another grand view, Station Square – a vast open space flanked on three sides by a reflective gridded office building which feels like a scene from Jacques Tati's modernist satire *Playtime* (1967). A circular clock on a round steel post, marking the city centre and by implication your place in the cosmic order, also aligns with the start of Midsummer Boulevard, which runs straight and broad for one-and-a-half miles

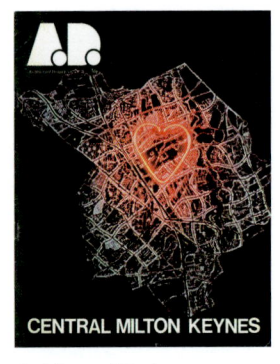

Architectural Design, 1974, one of three issues dedicated to Milton Keynes in the 1970s. This edition, with a cover by Minale Tattersfield (appointed to design a brand for the entire city), includes an interview with Terence Conran offering advice on the design of MK's shopping centre following his success as the founder of Habitat

Opposite: Milton Keynes Development Corporation architects' department at Wavendon Tower, Milton Keynes, early 1970s

Gardens, Grids and Ghosts

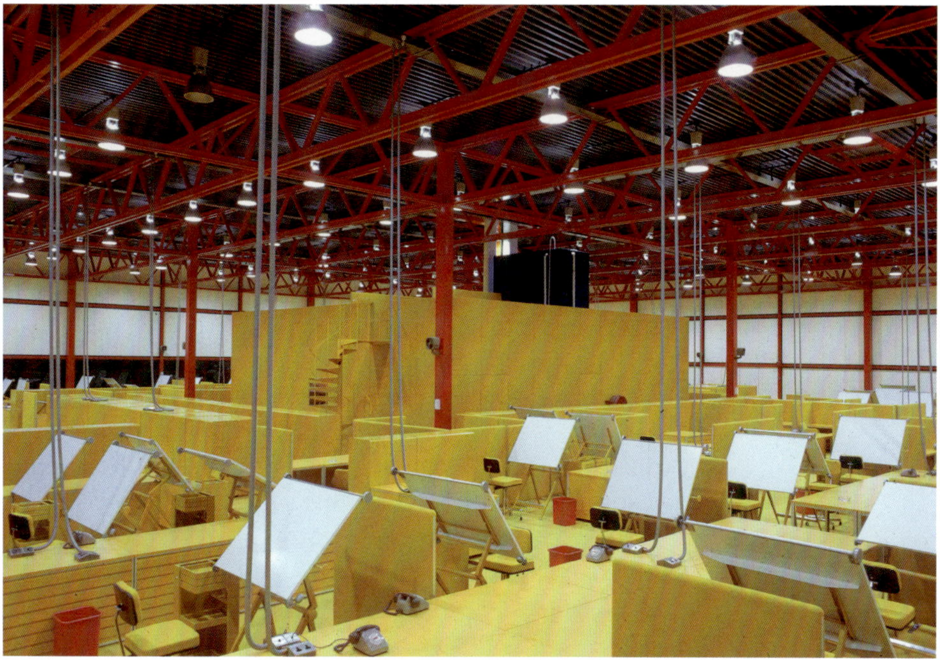

to Campbell Park at the other end. This boulevard is the central axis of the grid that makes up Central Milton Keynes (CMK), the *bastide*-like core of this landscape-city, and forms a picturesque unity of town, roads, parkland and boulevards also named after old English, pre-Christian landscapes: Avebury and Silbury.

CMK's grid is rigid and orthogonal, but the rest of the city relies on a softer order, with roads mediating between iso-curves and other folds in the former fields and pastures. As a result, the system of roads and mini-roundabouts, for which the town still maintains a certain notoriety, is infinitely scalable and connects a celestial alignment with the precise placement of paving slabs. Here, as elsewhere in Milton Keynes, is a municipal utopia, its character carefully planned by design standards and prototypical elements, from playscapes and typography to infrastructure, and all described in the local planning department's *Infrastructure Pack* (1975), much like the pattern books of the decorous Georgian city of the eighteenth century, which specified every architectural feature, from fanlights and railings to sash windows. But Milton Keynes remains a fundamentally social project, whose utopianism depended just as readily on its public spaces as on its catalogue of designed elements.

The city continues to challenge many of our assumptions of the nature of a modern city, not least because it is a landscape structure more than it is metropolitan; layered rather than zoned; synthetic and organic; structured around long axes laid over undulating topography that prevent grand vistas. Conceived as a totality, Milton Keynes is in many ways the legacy of experimental postwar British architecture, especially in housing, even if like all utopias its most audacious experiment remains unbuilt. At the heart of the city was to be the City Club, a cultural and leisure centre on an epic scale which has long hovered over the city's imagination and sense of itself, with a sprawling programme of sport, arts, markets, leisure and community services, anticipating today's eco-cultural lifestyle of choice by half a century.

Although its roots can be found in an English political and landscape tradition, and in the great Georgian architectural projects in London, Bath and Edinburgh, the centre of Milton Keynes also reveals profound influences of the American city and its theories of equity through mobility. Here it is worth remembering that Thomas Jefferson, author of the territorial grid with the Land Ordinance of 1785, was one of many political visitors to Stowe, and used the model to reimagine the territory west of the Mississippi as reducible to a vast new conceptual grid regardless of established settlements. From state boundaries to the perimeter of an individual farmstead, this grid inscribed the freedoms of the Declaration of Independence in an American landscape yet to be settled. At least Milton Keynes absorbed ancient villages to gently deform the grid around their village greens, pubs and chapels. In 1733 it had already physically defined the new city of Savannah, Georgia, as a colonial new town laid out in a rational alignment of building plots, squares and gardens like a perfect kind of chequerboard. A similar tension between individual perspective and collective purpose is constantly present in Milton Keynes, just as it is impossible to separate the urban from the bucolic, or the technocratic from the psychedelic. These multiplicities may also explain how CMK's grid could so easily pass from the original social mission of the 1960s to the individualised laissez-faire of Margaret Thatcher's 1980s; the grid remains open and free to inhabit according to any point of view.

Jacoby Glass

Milton Keynes, 2019, by Iwan Baan

At the turn of the nineteenth century, England's evolving landscape tradition adopted the ideals of the picturesque and in the process its grand gardens were recast as narratives of framed images that always privileged an individual's point of view. Emblematic of this change, it became fashionable to carry a pocket-sized dark mirror to frame a pleasant landscape as if it were a painting by Claude Lorrain. This so-called Claude Glass, the reflecting surface of which could create multiple pictures in the palm of the hand, was later succeeded by Hollywood, with postwar cinema projecting the idea of individual freedom framed from the moving car, an American landscape passing across the windscreen and receding perspectives in the rearview mirror. In this sense, the picturesque grew to be much more than simply a period in the history of landscape; it cemented the individual's point of view as the centre of modern experience and meaning.

Milton Keynes revived its own use of the picturesque before it was even built. The Development Corporation, commissioned by the great architectural illustrator Helmut Jacoby to promote the emerging city in a series of views that situated aspirational young families enjoying newfound leisure in the matrix of a city grid and orbital landscapes. In Jacoby's most famous rendering, from 1971, we see the city from aerial perspective. A helicopter (somewhat ambiguously departing the city) fills the lower left corner of the image, its rotors and landing gear representing a kind of contemporary recasting of the twisted figures leaning against and ancient tree typical of standard picturesque paintings, while, again like earlier precedents, the top section of the image fades into white, leaving the horizon empty. At the bottom of the drawing, darker and more defined, Jacoby outlines the distinctive circles and cones of Campbell Park below the perspectival grid of CMK. Sometimes described as a sculpture park, but more accurately conceived as a sculpture in its own right (like Stowe), Campbell Park directly evoked the English landscape garden with an assortment of grotto, temples and obelisks aligning directly with the clock in Station Square through Midsummer Boulevard.

Milton Keynes in 1990, by Helmut Jacoby, 1971

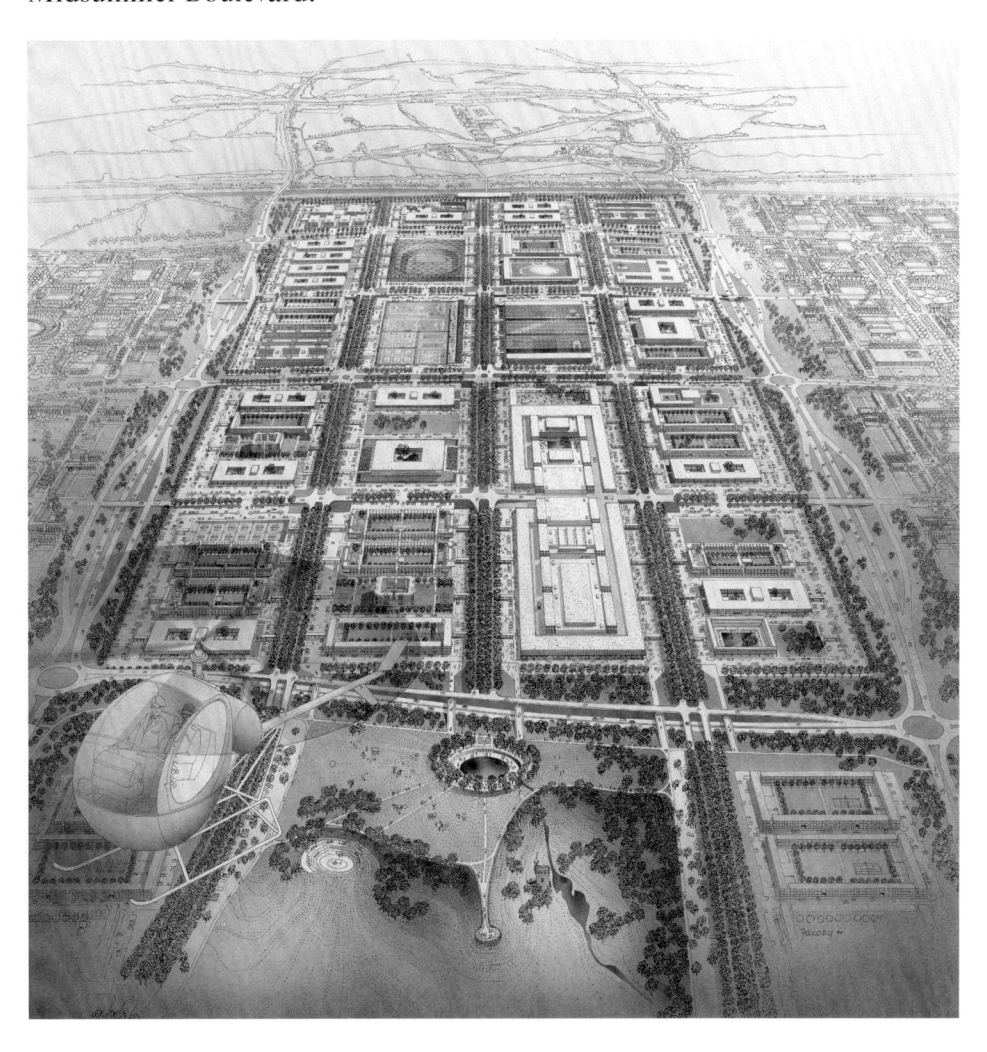

Mies's Ghost

In the middle of Jacoby's image lies the crowning architectural achievement of CMK: the 750-metre-long Shopping Building. Part Crystal Palace, part Miesian pavilion, its scale cannot conceal its type, which essentially belongs to landscape and leisure, albeit with powerful consumerist benefits. Architects educated immediately after the Second World War were typically encouraged to choose whether to follow Mies van der Rohe or Le Corbusier, so dominant was their presence in architecture schools. Here, the choice is clear, for it is the ghost of Mies that marches along the exquisite rhythms of steel and glass, in step with every paving slab and tree.

Mies van der Rohe had two distinct careers. In the 1920s and 1930s his European work was sensual, crafted and luxurious. Derek Walker, chief architect and planner for Milton Keynes, included the plan of the celebrated 1929 German Pavilion in Barcelona in an array of images underpinning the city's design in the early 1970s. It is telling that he chose a project that is in many ways a landscape more than it is a building. When Mies migrated to the US in the late 1930s he reinvented his architecture for the American landscape and the American city. Out went the lavish materials and crafted details, in came industrial steel profiles and external structures, reaching into a space bigger than any European imagination could ever contain. (Some of the architects working on Milton Keynes had worked in Mies's office and had brought back working drawings for a school in Chicago that served as a go-to rule book when the enormity of designing the town needed guidance – just look at the roof of the city's bus station for a more literal demonstration of a Miesian influence.)

The abstract reduction of Mies's American work, together with ideas surrounding West Coast mobility, were relayed back to Europe and refracted by radical architects using serial repetition and grids as sites

Opposite: MK Gallery by 6a architects from Campbell Park, 2019

for utopian visions, such as Superstudio's *Continuous Monument* (1969), which projected an infinite grid circumnavigating the world. In Britain, however, technology provided the route to utopia, not least in Archigram's *Walking Cities* (1964) and in Cedric Price and Joan Littlewood's *Fun Palace* (1961). Combining ideas embedded within a landscape garden tradition (passing through Victorian pleasure gardens) with the grids of the American city and a sprinkling of English utopian high-tech created an extremely modern, even postmodern, collage. Add to that a multiplicity of other historic architectural and landscape references and stimuli beyond the visual (from pop culture to welfare state politics), and the idea of a city of the perpetual future emerges, even half a century after it began.

From CMK to MKG

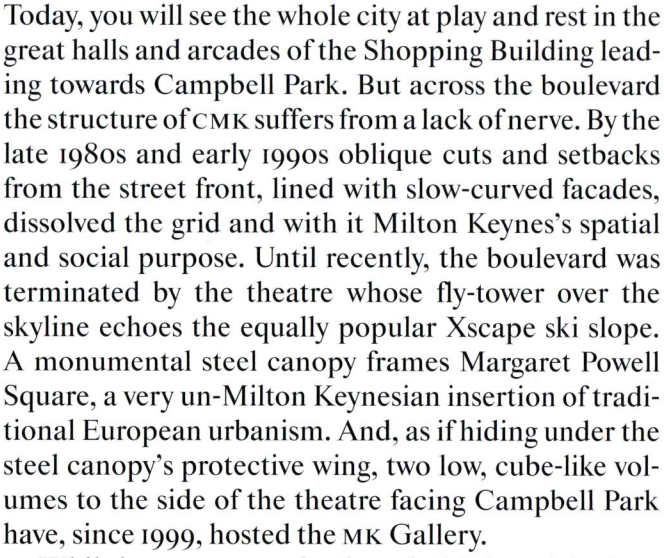

Today, you will see the whole city at play and rest in the great halls and arcades of the Shopping Building leading towards Campbell Park. But across the boulevard the structure of CMK suffers from a lack of nerve. By the late 1980s and early 1990s oblique cuts and setbacks from the street front, lined with slow-curved facades, dissolved the grid and with it Milton Keynes's spatial and social purpose. Until recently, the boulevard was terminated by the theatre whose fly-tower over the skyline echoes the equally popular Xscape ski slope. A monumental steel canopy frames Margaret Powell Square, a very un-Milton Keynesian insertion of traditional European urbanism. And, as if hiding under the steel canopy's protective wing, two low, cube-like volumes to the side of the theatre facing Campbell Park have, since 1999, hosted the MK Gallery.

While its programme has been bold, the original MK Gallery building never quite managed to key itself into the original vision of the city. It departs from the great CMK plan not because of its modest scale, although it could easily fit into one of the many halls in the shopping centre, but because it occupies its site without registering CMK's Cartesian order. And yet still it has reserved its place. More recently, in 2012, the gallery initiated a programme of expansion to double the exhibition spaces and add an audience of café visitors that was always anticipated but never quite realised, as well as a learning space and multipurpose auditorium. And in the city's tradition of multidisciplinary integration, a reinvented City Club, created by artists Gareth Jones and Nils Norman, extended the gallery into the city beyond, restoring and renewing Milton Keynesian ideals and design history into the public realm – play and leisure once more being central to the art.

Today, at the end of Midsummer Boulevard a new polished and gridded stainless steel box stands as large as the plot and budget allowed. A large circle,

Gareth Jones, Nils Norman and 6a architects, *City Club Conceptual Model*, 2015

Gardens, Grids and Ghosts

borrowed from Campbell Park, dominates the centre of the grid in a simple geometric encounter with CMK. The city-landscape idea replayed on the outside facing the park continues within; openings between three original galleries are realigned with the larger gallery in the new building, creating an internal axis that extends outwards towards the city and the park in equally sized windows. On either side of the white-cube axis, City Club merges the building with the landscape in colour, materiality and use; education and play escape into open space to the south, while shop and café extend with high-tech accents onto Midsummer Boulevard to the north. Like CMK, the new gallery plays on a background of rational planning overlaid with a narrative about the city itself and its multiple origins in the English landscape and psyche, the invention of leisure, American modernity and many other ideals best told by the architectures of City Club.

Above the galleries, in the auditorium, the whiteness turns pastoral. Douglas fir plywood dressed over grid timber studwork containing acoustic insulation rises to meet a high-tech ceiling of exposed steel structure and services. A curtain striped in City Club's

Gareth Jones and Nils Norman, *City Club Urban Planning Tool Kit*, 2015, colour chart from Habitat catalogue, 1974

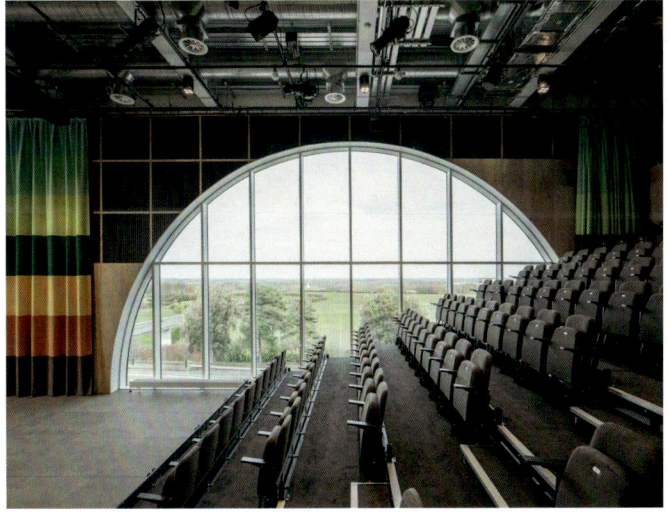

MK Gallery by 6a architects, interior – café (above) and auditorium (left), featuring *City Club* by Gareth Jones and Nils Norman, 2019

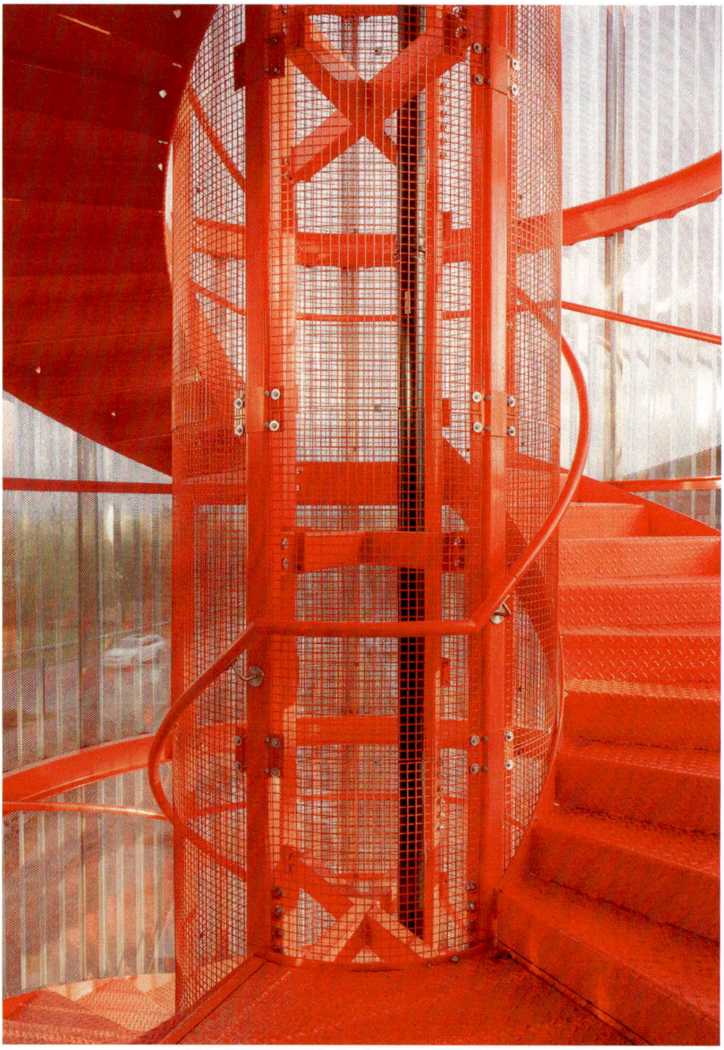

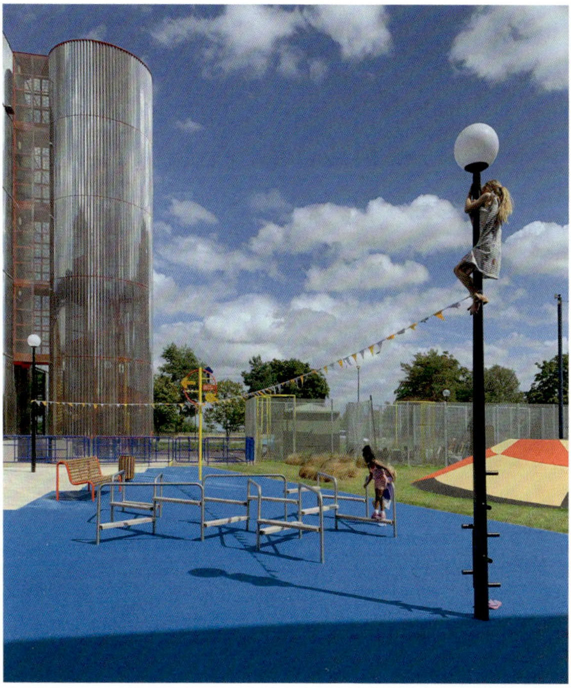

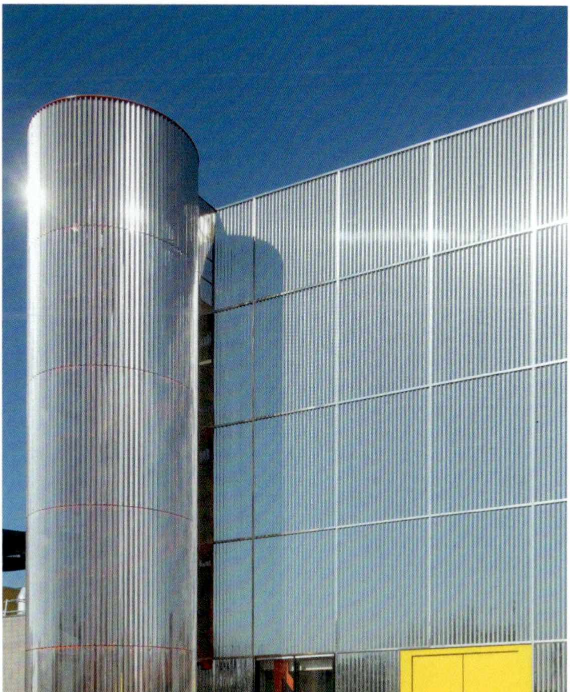

sedimented landscape colours reveals the semi-circular picture window offering a fine prospect over Campbell Park and beyond. Without virtue or vice, here is MK's contemporary grotto. The proto-museum at the centre of the English Landscape Garden has turned into the public reality promised in Milton Keynes's social mission, an arching panorama that surveys all before it, and an echo to the same promise recommended by John Woolridge in his *Systema Horti-Culturae*, or *The Art of Gardening* (1677):

Previous spread:
MK Gallery by 6a architects, with external stair (left) featuring *City Club* by Gareth Jones and Nils Norman and *City Club Playscape* (top right), by Gareth Jones and Nils Norman, 2019

MK Gallery under construction, 2018

Gardens, Grids and Ghosts

May you make a place of repose, cool and fresh in the greatest heats. It may be arched...and may you have all those before mentioned water-works, for your own or your friends' divertisements.

Working at Home Like Everyone Else

@officialnormanfoster
20 March 2020

Scrolling through Instagram, a photograph taken over the shoulder of Norman Foster at his desk catches my eye: '@officialnormanfoster: Working at home like everyone else.' As if. It is sweet though. Cross-country skiing marathon in St Moritz, cycling across the Golden Gate Bridge in Lycra on a carbon fibre bike or designing a museum in *insert any major city here*. Five hundred and twenty thousand followers. Lots of classic cars. He just loves life. A good life. An amazing life.

I notice that he is left-handed like me. Lefties notice each other more quickly than others. On his desk, A4 papers of drawings, images and texts. To his right, his signature inclined drawing board. In front of him, pages describing the project at hand are folded over the corner staple to reveal a pale timber-framed interior with ceiling spiralling towards a central oculus. NF is drawing in his sketchbook. Just beyond are two sheaths of hand sketches pinched together by a central bulldog clip. They look like typical archi-sketches. But no one is as clear as NF. He sketches diagrams like proof of the future; the sun is here, fresh air moves along twisting arrows, people, structure, space – all will be harmony. A little further, past the sheets of poetic technologic, *A Bigger Picture*, the 2012 catalogue of David Hockney's homecoming exhibition at the Royal Academy. On the cover is a red tree trunk in simplified perspective under big green leaves in the foreground. The artist came back to East Yorkshire to capture his native landscape. I flick through our copy. Polychromatic landscapes painted in the open air. Fields so English no amount of Californian luminosity could disguise them. Stop at the spread on 184–85: a charcoal drawing on each page, *Autumn Thixendale, October 18th, 2008* on the left, *19th* on the right. Three *great* trees. Multicentenary at least. Trees have become the unexpected protagonists of Covid spring. Will they remain so in the autumn?

Like all prophets of the future, NF and DH are sentimental. They must know one another. Eighty-two and eighty-four. Working-class kids in the north of England caught by the bright light of 1960s America. Los Angeles pools and palms for DH, Yale seriousness for NF. DH's glamorous modernity splashed across canvases is always melancholic especially in Los Angeles sunshine. Norman's invention cannot be tainted. Nodes and vectors make the space frame for utopia. The heavy smoker, romantic contrarian or the healthy option.

Beyond the desk, a white Eames chair pulled up to a table whose glossy surface suggests Jacobsen marble. The walls are white. The window in the centre is surprisingly small. I can't tell what is outside and therefore where we are. What is revealed is an exterior of timber shingles. But this is not the firm's famously shingle-clad Chesa Futura in St Moritz – wrong kind of window. Still, probably alpine.

Despite not working inside one of his buildings, his architecture is everywhere. Beside the window, three architectural models are displayed like framed pictures of children. To the right is the Hong Kong Shanghai Bank (1979–86), standing about five feet tall. Later renamed HSBC, the red and white logo has been added to both building and model. To the left, a model of the Hearst Tower in New York (2000–06) and one of the Gherkin in London (1997–2004). NF works away in his pale blue cashmere jumper, seemingly oblivious to the three late-modern monuments of global capitalism in front of him, each one brilliant in its own right. I will need to charge up to write a worthy critique another time. Not that they need another one, but they certainly deserve it. They are all empty now. Will they ever be refilled to the same capacity? The models are covered by Perspex, Covid's new vernacular. Only the Gherkin case cover reveals a satisfying reflection of the room beyond: a Nomos table (1986) with its lunar landing module feet. NF works on undistracted. He is an optimist, just not quite like everyone else. Fifty-six thousand, three hundred and eighty likes.

Juergen on a Plate

Why are you so fucking nervous? I don't know. I'm not used to being photographed, let alone by Juergen Teller. He was shooting a series of male portraits for *Arena Homme+*. All kinds of men: artists, actors, porn stars, models, writers, critics, designers of every kind – landscape, fashion, graphics and me, an architect.

When I arrived at his studio, we went straight to the kitchen for coffee. Debris was all around: clothes, boots, props, plates. While chatting about this and that, Juergen told me how Adrian Searle had stumbled wearing the previous model's silver platform boots and sprained his ankle, resulting in a portrait of him lying on his back, swollen foot raised on a chair. So, yes, I was nervous. I had no idea what would happen, only that anything could happen. Juergen picked up his camera and cigarettes and walked out to the walled garden that separated the kitchen from the central studio space. Once he was nicotined-up, we went inside the studio. A strip of rough timber boards crosses the studio floor, covering a trench with pipes and wires. Today the trench was open for maintenance. Juergen told me, the architect, to sit in the trench. He placed a small figurine of himself wearing his signature fluorescent shorts and orange puffer on a plate next to me, making me feel greyer than usual. We talked about the space, the gardens, the light passing through the structure above. I waved my hands upwards, mirroring my legs dangling below ground. We were back to the conversations we'd had for years while designing the studio. Then, calmly, Juergen said, that's it. I've got what I need. It was over.

For decades, Juergen has been making portraits around the world to find his subjects in situ. His studio is anywhere except a traditional photographic studio. A hotel room can be as natural as a forest and an urban street can be more intimate than a bedroom. His subject simply needs a connection and a habitat. Whether for fashion where the habitat can be a fantasy, or a portrait where it is found in the everyday space.

Back in spring 2011, Juergen took me and my partner Steph Macdonald on a walk along one of the most ordinary streets in west London. Beyond the bustle of the city centre, but not yet reaching leafy suburbia, it might be described as dull except for the raised motorway flying overhead, executed with all the charm of a 1970s highway planner. Thanks to JG Ballard's *Concrete Island*, the Westway has been rehabilitated as a monument to dystopian modernity and makes a fertile place for Juergen's eye. On the ground, its lack of charm is matched by a quiet industry. Electrical wholesalers, tyres and paint in bulk occupy low metal warehouses. Juergen had found a narrow space formerly occupied by a building contractor, sixty metres long by seven metres wide and entirely enclosed by walls. It's said that these long thin plots were common in the neighbourhood during the nineteenth century, used as laundries operated by the Portuguese community who still run the busy restaurants and bars in nearby Golborne Road.

Juergen moved into the neighbourhood in the early 90s, which was, at the time, the epicentre of Britpop. But by 2011 London's creative energy had migrated east. The shift suited his own desire for a kind of retreat where he could make a world unto itself, a little paradise away from distraction, like the walled gardens of antiquity. Juergen made few specific demands, except that it should be a place where people might come to him, where he could think, make photographs, exhibitions and books. Natural light and gardens.

It is easy to recognise a photograph by Juergen Teller. There are the tell-tale aesthetics of bright golden sunlight or a shock of flash that casts minutely offset shadow line. And vivid colour of every hue subdued in a nicotine-tinted haze. Or jaunty informality capturing otherworldly glamour. While these are present in many images and copied in even more, they mask more profound truths. His images may originate with a specific subject – be it a person, garment or bag – but the narrative

Juergen on a Plate

transcends the immediate focus. Juergen's work possesses an inherent expansiveness, fusing the individual in their environment. His candid conversations ease the situation into an all-encompassing atmosphere that envelops the subject. And the more outlandish the situation, the more real the human within. Sitter and scene collapse into one as light hits the back of the camera. Kate Moss on a farm, snugly tucked up in a wheelbarrow, his daughter Lola emerging from a pond in unreal stillness, or David Hockney, reclining in his own ash, surrounded by wilting flowers – all look as true and beautiful as any heavenly creature painted in paradise.

Juergen's eye-hand magic captures the fleeting moments of our nature forever. The trivial conversations preceding the shoot are there to find one's place and for Juergen to find mood or humour. Famously, this can happen in seconds. The irrepressible grin across Yves Saint Laurent's face was caught the moment the doors opened; a shoot finished before it had even started. Other images gestate over years, their roots deepening through mutual trust. Pictures of Kate Moss and Naomi Campbell are iconic of their times and with each passing decade transform into documentaries of lives lived in augmented reality. Charlotte Rampling or Vivienne Westwood are the longest shoots of all as photographer and subject go in search of each other in hotel rooms, baroque museum interiors, car parks with caviar or football to pass the time. The playfulness of so many of Juergen's images binds him and his subjects in a shared conspiracy. Wild play is the perfect cover for pathos. All the exuberance in the world cannot cover the trials of life. Each photograph is a fragment of a longer tale. When the story is extended, sometimes for a hundred pages or more for publication, bags and clothes disappear into bedrooms, swimming pools, landscapes or infrastructure – like the Westway at the end of the road, which embraces all things and actions below its concrete wings.

We started designing the studio with a simple premise: to use the length of the plot to generate a natural spatial sequence from street to hinterland. Walls of varying height and material separate Juergen's space from adjacent gardens, an electrical substation, apartments and offices that lay out of sight. Light had to come from above and views were created within. We arranged three identical buildings set between gardens along the sixty-metre walled strip. Garden (with parking spot), building, garden, building, garden, building, garden (wilderness). A repeating rhythm of deep concrete beams marching overhead ties the walls together and filters daylight from above. Spaces unfold, exchanging light and dark, inside with outside until they all become one. Let the demands of real life take care of the rest.

London has never had a dominant architectural language and has never accepted grand organising masterplans. It is built eccentrically in competitive collisions and accidents that reveal an unruly temperament like Juergen's. There was no obvious precedent to design this studio, but the galleries at the rear of the architect John Soane's house, on Lincoln's Inn Fields, provided a suitably oblique reference. It is the archetypical London studio. Suites of windowless rooms and micro courtyards, buried in the city fabric far away from public view, hide the most unlikely and sublime London light. Lanterns push upwards to pull daylight downwards softly over ancient architectural fragments that fill the space to the brim. In the picture gallery, Canaletto, Turner, Hogarth and Piranesi extend ruinous fragments beyond the walls, merging ancient ruins at one with nature with London's squalid eighteenth-century streets. We never shared our Soane-ian thoughts with Juergen, fearing he would reject pretentiousness and arcane Englishness, but the idea of a building gradually ruined by natural forces seemed to suit Juergen and our times. The built spaces would be raw, precise and crafted before being gradually taken over by wild gardens.

The first building standing on the street is the most public. Deliveries, administration, post-production and archive. Then a garden leads to the central building, a single double-height space with flank walls of raw, off-white blockwork separated by glass walls looking onto the gardens. Through the studio, the next garden, a little wilder than the first, takes you to the last building, more intimate in scale and use. A kitchen and a library. Sometime later in the design process, Juergen asked for a sauna, declaring with little discernible irony that *I am German, provincial and successful. I have a Mercedes and a sauna.* That's me told. (The Mercedes and sauna have, of course, featured in his work – all tax deductible.) And, right at the back, a world away from the city life, the smallest garden is the most untamed. Tetrapanax plants with hand-like leaves as large as open umbrellas engulf the fire escape in wilderness.

Work continued; compromises with neighbours were reached, delays endured and details agreed. Juergen never had much patience for plans and even less for the slowness of architecture, although, as might be expected, he has an incredibly quick eye for space and proportion. Busy with new projects of his own, he was losing heart with this one. But luckily, with the site acquired and permission granted, it was not so easy to stop.

Finally, on the day construction is to start, I receive a text from Juergen: *Been to site with my camera full of excitement to start the workers shoot. Fucking no one there!* Juergen is often full of excitement. He shares his thoughts and memories freely, which invites us to share our own. Any subject will do but football never fails to energise. Just don't ask forgiveness the day after a Bayern loss. Trivia mixes with the personal until Juergen knows what he wants, and you trust him to find it. It is how he does what he does. But there is more to it than peaks of excitement; while the sun shines bright on fashion shoots, there is melancholic shade for portraits.

Once the builders did arrive, Juergen was on site to shoot them at work and occasionally in prayer. Sometimes he would add a fashion shoot to steel, cement mixers and all manner of construction site debris before bemused/amused contractors. His yoga teacher, in Lycra and hi-vis jacket, clutches Prada bags while standing barefoot in poses few of us can reach on steady ground. Despite the misfit of just about everything, the situation is balanced and playful. Muddy browns and dirty greys wrap around shots of purple and poise. The planting of the garden provides another kind of show. Cranes flying a multi-stemmed amelanchier tree over rooftops and groups of men wrestling it into the fresh earth were treated and photographed like great choreography. Whether model or builder, Juergen shows each body and soul fully engaged in its tasks. A tree in the air is no more out of place than the yoga teacher's feet in the mud. The studio-garden continues to grow in the background of so many pictures. Unlike a photograph, a building is never finished. As building works end, decay begins.

The studio is forever in a constant cycle of maintenance, repair and seasonal renewal. Ground cover and climbers grow in the gardens, designed by Dan Pearson, each species blossoming in turn to fill all the seasons with the natural order of flora making robust habitat in urban wastelands. The remains of previous constructions were incorporated as a reminder that we are never the first to occupy space. We simply follow what came before and precede unknown others. Juergen's construction site images would soon swap the hi-vis accessories of industry for more tranquil surroundings. Photographs, like the gardens, measure the passing of time.

Juergen moved into the studio in late spring, starting the new era with his portraits for *Arena Homme+*. Despite the trauma of recent transplantation, the amelanchier tree was in full white blossom, which became a fitting crown over Dan Pearson's head. The graphic designer Peter Miles, also standing in the garden, plate in one hand, tennis racket in the other, looks pleadingly to the sky. Behind him the fragment of concrete structure from the previous building, which rises in the shape of a T, becomes the stage for the curator Francesco Bonami, who holds another white plate in sympathy with the neighbours' satellite dishes that poke over the wall. In fact, the only thing connecting all the portraits is place and plate. *Teller* is plate in German. Juergen was signing his work and new studio anywhere light would catch a little texture or colour.

The issue came out with nudes alongside the outlandishly dressed up and simply overdressed, like me. Each of us finding a place under a tree, up a ladder, surrounded by tools or in a trench. Some found their way out onto the street among the sandbags left over from construction, and one even escaped to the sandy horse ground below the Westway. Flicking through the magazine trying to read Juergen's story of men, the picture of Vivienne Westwood's partner, Andreas Kronthaler, lying nude on a rug resting his shoulders against the raw blockwork wall stopped the narrative flow. The rug itself is woven with one of Juergen's famous nudes of Vivienne in delicate shades of off-white and orange. Andreas is compressed in the very bottom of the image. At the very top, cool blue daylight falls through slim beams across the blockwork wall, grading to warm yellow when it reaches his body, which lies there, knee up, just like Vivienne. Among the wildness of this first series in the studio, Juergen finds a moment of intimacy. The space above Andreas and Vivienne witnesses their profound kinship on the ground. Juergen's double portrait merges play with truth.

Later, in good biblical fashion, Juergen re-enacted Cranach's double portrait of Adam and Eve in the Garden of Eden. Animals soon followed: a donkey, a dinosaur, giant frogs, snails, worms. And a fox sharing a plate of milk with Charlotte Rampling in the garden. Chaos and calm alternate. Fashion shoots pass by like a circus through town, while portraits retreat into monastic solitude and another fragment is lost under plants.

More than a decade has passed since that first walk in the shadow of the Westway. Juergen has not stopped travelling, but the world has also come to him in the studio. Hundreds if not thousands of pictures are out there, forming great ensemble casts or solitary moments. I can locate each one exactly, from the fall of light or a leaf growing through the cracks. Images I first saw in conversations full of excitement naturally pass into memory. Standing in the garden on a plastic mat marked 'wet grass', Virgil Abloh pretends to water the plants before sweating it out in the sauna. Vivienne Westwood hides behind the orange-browns of a huge tetrapanax leaf wilting. The pictures are so full of life it is hard to believe it is over so soon, too soon. All that remain are memories kept alive in conversations, which sometimes also lead to a photograph.

First published in the catalogue essay accompanying the exhibition *I Need to Live* by Juergen Teller, Grand Palais Ephémère, Paris, 2023. Catalogue published by Steidl, Göttingen, 2024

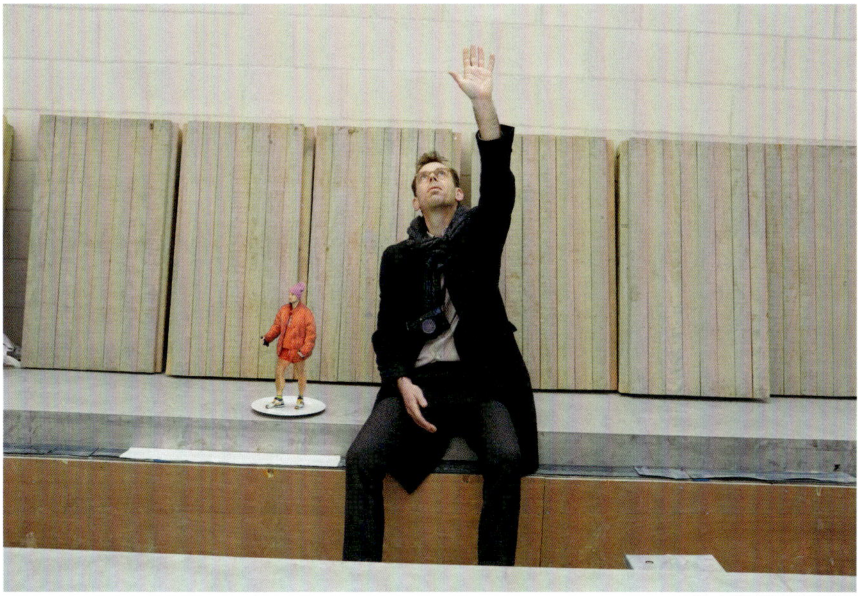

Figure of Speech n.1
Assonance
Virgil Abloh
Jun - 22 Sep
MCA Chicago
220 E Chicago
60611 Chicago,
"WET GRASS"

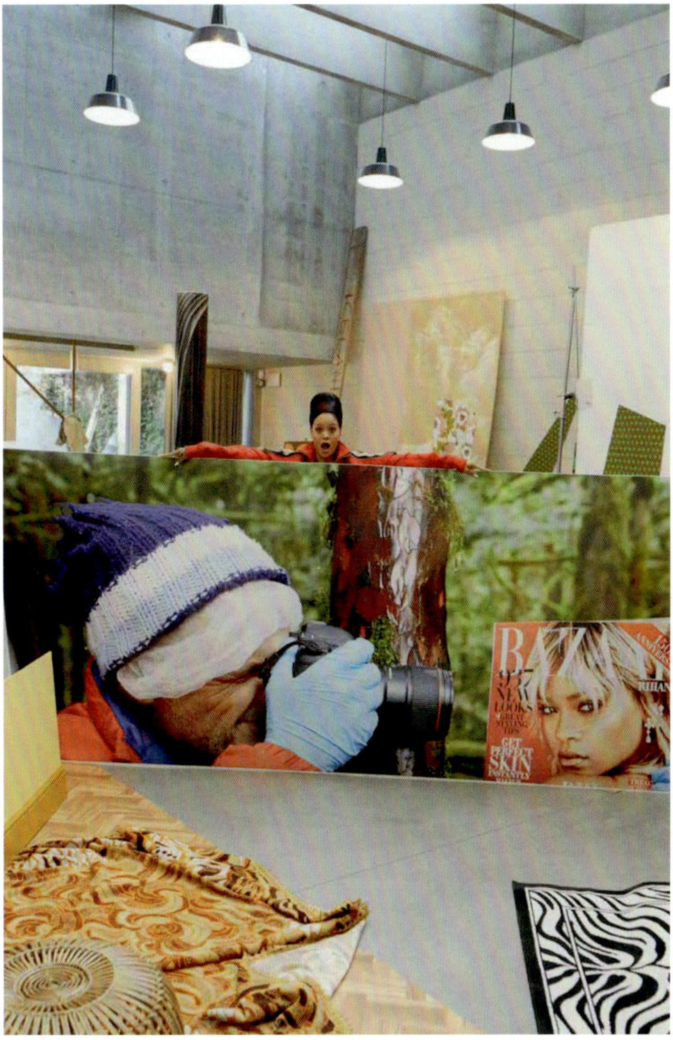
SKIN

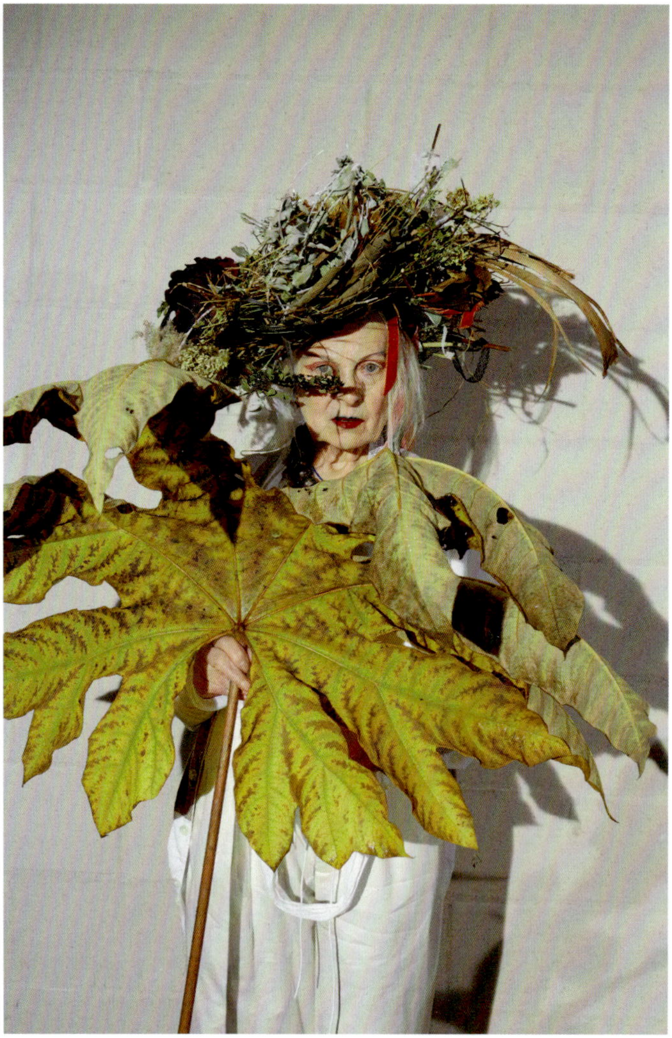

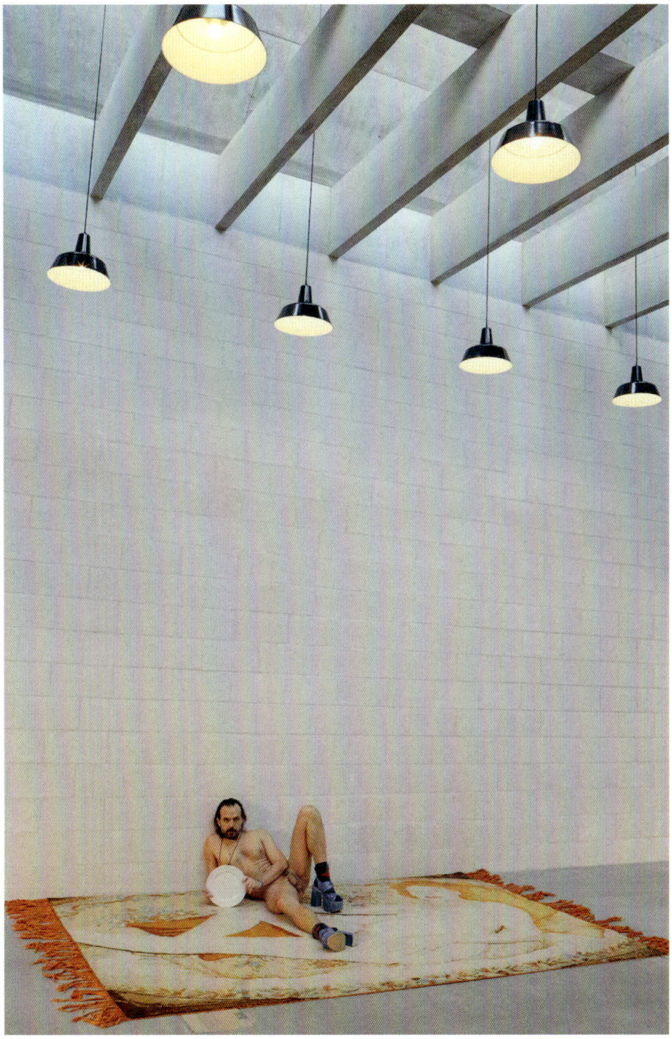

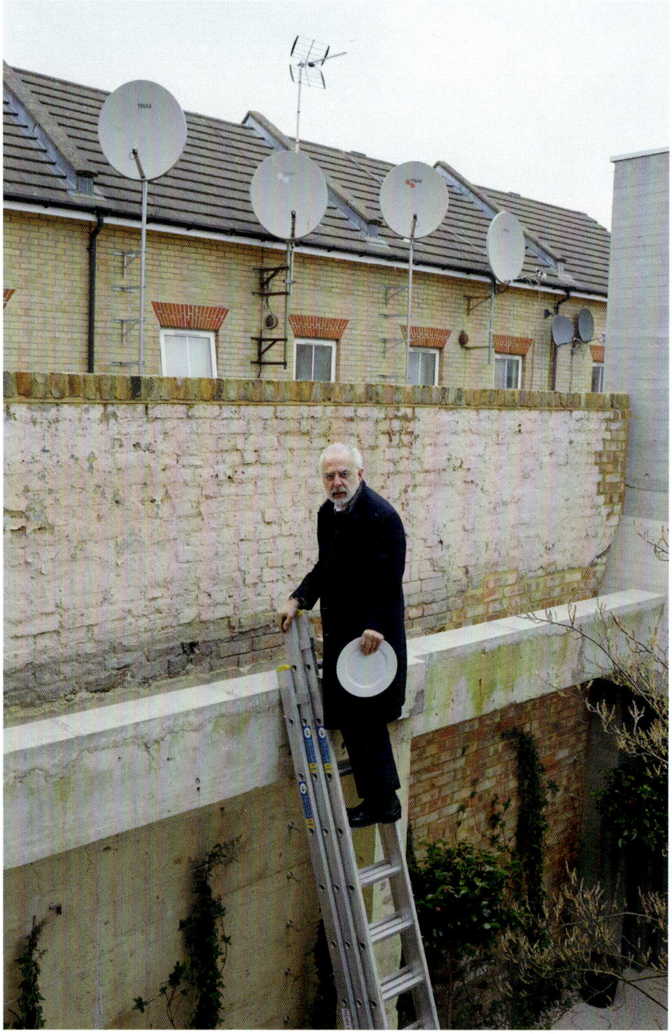

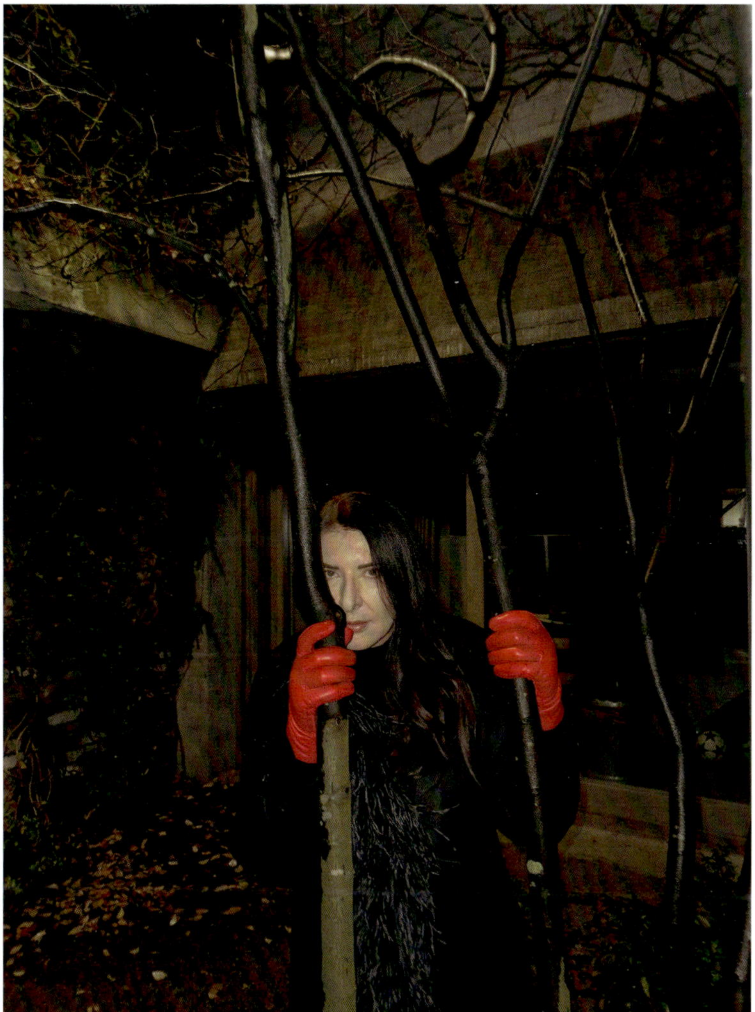

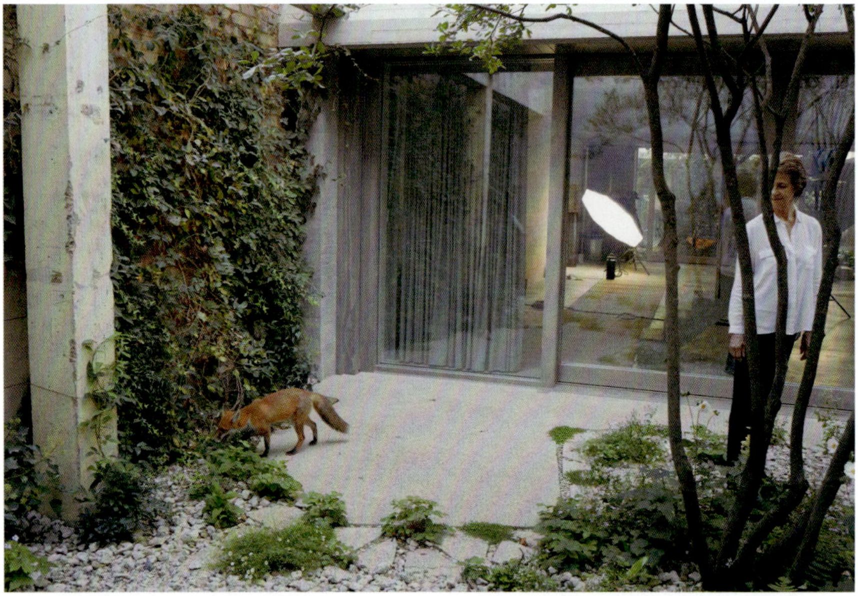

Tough Love

Architects love gardening but mainly as a metaphor. Notions of growth, decay and renewal enrich the discipline with poetic abstractions that help us imagine other worlds, other ways of making and designing. The parallels between architecture and the garden are ancient. To imagine the building as a garden or the garden as a house has accompanied both disciplines since the mythical wall enclosed a patch of ground for cultivation. More recent architect-gardener metaphors have introduced the much-needed values of care and caution to temper the revolutionary zeal of modernism or the defensive retreat of postmodernism. The architect's metaphorical garden stands for an idealised nature, a benign environment away from the violence and cruelties of everyday life where the human spirit not only finds solace but also myth, allegory, politics and even satire. The garden is the world in living form yet protected from its total force. In the architect's metaphorical garden there is no late frost to kill the spring shoots, there are no droughts or floods, only a giving nature. The metaphorical garden also conveniently needs no work.

The gardener is the guardian of the metaphor; a gentle soul who will protect and enhance architecture's perfection in nature. The metaphor is sadly mostly visual, which is why the picturesque is an idea most associated with landscape. And while it is only a short chapter in landscape history, its conceptual action was with us long, long ago and still remains.

But have you seen a gardener pruning in February? It is a scene of shocking violence and resilience. Cutting back is brutal, almost cruel if you do not know the inner life of trees. Work is hard. The trees are bare, the air is cold, earth is heavy and waterlogged if not frozen solid, birdsong still far away. Why is so much harm brought upon these fragile stems? The real gardener cuts the metaphor just like they cut the excess branches that will enable the new life-force of spring. The wise gardener is tough in thought and action. Feet on the ground, or in the ground to be precise, the year ahead will pass through their rough fingertips. Communicating is direct and unsentimental. The gardener is in nature, not looking at nature. Their actions are natural and far from gentle. Cut, weed, thin. Sow, spread, till. The work is decisive, easily upsetting the architect's inclination for compositional hesitations. It is marked by embodied knowledge and trust in what has yet to come.

The real gardener is the opposite of the architect or the metaphorical gardener. They do not build, they do not fix things in time or place. They strip to raw structure and redistribute so that the garden may grow back stronger. They may use a plan, but it is just that: a plan, an intention. The real design has already been done in genetic codes for growth, in the sedimentation of organic and mineral matter into geology and in the movement of clouds, rain, winds and sunshine. That is the gardener's meta-architecture. Composition will be completed during the seasons of plenty and their busy crowds. Birds and insects will buzz and sing as they work, guided and seduced by colour and scent. People will wander and wonder, picnic and sleep. But storms and gales will come and the gardener has to prepare for them too as they will not spare the weak. The gardener's task is physically tough yet full of unspoken communication. As we search for ways to respond to the big questions of our time, it is right to look to gardening for new and natural ways of working and communicating with the world. And the architect is right to imagine gardening as an act of love. We just have to accept how tough that love needs to be.

First published in *Ganz: Contemporary Swiss Landscape Architecture* by Daniel Ganz, Hochparterre, Zurich, 2021

Tom Emerson is an architect. In 2001 he co-founded London-based 6a architects with Stephanie Macdonald. Since 2010 he has been professor of architecture at ETH Zurich.

Thank you Steph for collaborating in everything within and beyond these pages

Thank you to the team at 6a architects, especially Karolina Sznajder, John Ross, Owen Watson

Thank you to the artists and architects who created the work I have been fortunate to write about: Johan Dehlin, Monika Sosnowska, Nele Dechmann, Álvaro Siza, Daniel Ganz, Juergen Teller and Dovile Drizyte

To Carles Muro and Sónia Oliveira for inviting me to immerse in the archive of Álvaro Siza

To friends and critics Irénée Scalbert, Ingrid Schroeder, David Grandorge, Peter Carl and Edwin Heathcote, whose conversations have inspired, provoked and encouraged much more than this collection

To Richard Wentworth whose influence alone could fill a book

To my parents, Barbara and Michael, who never stop writing

To Laurie for imagination, wit and kindness

To Boris Gusic and Amy Perkins for inspiring years together at ETH and Martin Aeschbacher, Lucio Crignola, Lorenza Donati, Sonja Flury, Michelle Geilinger and Julius Henkel for taking it forward today

To the Department of Architecture at ETH Zurich for supporting this book

To the ETH students whose imaginations stimulated its writing

To Julie Cirelli at Park Books for making it happen

To Sarah Handelman for making it so much better

Thank you John Morgan, Teresa Lima, Adrien Vasquez for the art of book making and friendship

Picture credits

Framing Frank
Three buildings by Frank Gehry photographed by Johan Dehlin; pp.25-27 Indiana Avenue, Venice, California, 1979-80; pp.30-32 Spiller House, Venice, California, 1978-79

The Monika Papers
pp.37, 41-46 Monika Sosnowska, artist's models. Photo Eva Herzog, 2023; p.38 Monika Sosnowska, artist's model. Photo Juliusz Sokolowski, 2023; p.49 Monika Sosnowska, *Pipe*, 2016. Painted steel, 176 × 115 × 108 cm, Courtesy of The Artist and The Modern Institute/Toby Webster Ltd, Glasgow. Photo Max Slaven; p.50 Brassaï, *Sculptures Involontaires*, in *Minotaure* no. 3-4, 1933 ©RMN-Grand Palais

Cutting Corners
p.56 Centre d'Education FC Advan, Madagascar, by Nele Dechmann, 2020

Openings
p.70 Archive archt. Álvaro Siza. Col. Fundação de Serralves – Museu de Arte Contemporânea, Porto, Portugal. Donation 2021; p.71 Graphite and Indian ink on tracing paper, 61 × 65 cm. Scale 1:2. Archive archt. Álvaro Siza. Col. Fundação de Serralves – Museu de Arte Contemporânea, Porto, Portugal. Donation 2015; p.72 Archive archt. Álvaro Siza. Col. Fundação de Serralves – Museu de Arte Contemporânea, Porto, Portugal. Donation 2021; pp.74-75 Indian ink on tracing paper, 73.5 × 99.4 cm. Scales 1:50 and 1:5. Archive archt. Álvaro Siza. Col. Fundação de Serralves – Museu de Arte Contemporânea, Porto, Portugal. Donation 2015

Gardens, Grids and Ghosts
p.125 photo John Donat/RIBA Collections; p.128 Iwan Baan; p.129 ©Estate of Helmut Jacoby; p.131 Johan Dehlin; p.132 photo Gareth Jones; p.133 (middle and bottom) photos Johan Dehlin; p.134 photo Johan Dehlin; p.135 photos Tom Emerson; p.136 photo Martin Nässén

Juergen on a Plate
pp.153-160 Photographs by Juergen Teller; *Tom Emerson, Plates/Teller No.97*, London, 2016; *Virgil Abloh No.44*, London, 2018; *Self-portrait with Rihanna*, London, 2017; *Vivienne Westwood No.5*, London, 2020; *Andreas Kronthaler, Plates/Teller No.170*, London, 2016; *Francesco Bonami, Plates/Teller No.86*, London, 2016; *Marina Abramović No.11*, London, 2023; *Charlotte Rampling, a Fox, and a Plate No.7*, London, 2016

Tough Love
p.163 Daniel Ganz, Zurich, 2018. Photo Nemanja Zimonjic

Dirty Old River
by Tom Emerson

Edited by Sarah Handelman
Proofreading by Aimee Selby

Designed by John Morgan, Teresa Lima
and Adrien Vasquez, John Morgan studio

Image processing, printing, and binding
by die Keure, Belgium
Production by Sophie Kullmann

Typeset in Starling

© 2025 Tom Emerson, London
and Park Books, Zurich
© for the images: see image credits

Park Books
Niederdorfstrasse 54
8001 Zürich – Switzerland
park-books.com

Park Books is supported by the Federal Office of Culture with a general subsidy for the years 2021–2025.

All rights reserved. No part of this publication may be reproduced in any form by any electronic or mechanical means, including photocopying, recording, or information storage or retrieval, without permission in writing from the publisher.

ISBN 978-3-03860-404-4